TREASURES OF THE HOLY LAND

A Visit to the Places of Christian Origins

Veselin and Lydia W. Kesich

Illustrations by June Magaziner

St. Vladimir's Seminary Press
Crestwood, New York 10707
1985

TREASURES OF THE HOLY LAND

© copyright 1985

by

ST VLADIMIR'S SEMINARY PRESS

ISBN 0-88141-045-4

Library of Congress Cataloging-in-Publication Data

Kesich, Veselin, 1921—
    Treasures of the Holy Land.

Bibliography: p.
1. Israel—Description and travel—Guide-books.
2. West Bank—Description and travel—Guide-books.
3. Bible. N.T. Gospels—Geography. I. Kesich, Lydia W.,
    1928-   . II. Title.

DS103.K47   1985   915.694'0454   85-18403
ISBN 0-88141-045-4 (pbk.)

PRINTED IN THE UNITED STATES OF AMERICA
BY
EASTERN PRESS, INC.
NEW HAVEN, CT

Table of Contents

Part Three: THE JUDEAN DESERT

Afterword: The Holy Land and Modern Society

Preface

In late May and early June of 1981, we were able to visit Israel for the first time. During our two and a half weeks there we visited Nazareth and Galilee, the coastal towns of Caesarea and Akko, the Sea of Galilee and Capernaum, Caesarea Philippi, ancient Samaria and Nablus, Jerusalem, Bethlehem, Masada and the Dead Sea, and the Monastery of Mar Saba in the Judean desert. Knowledge of the country of Jesus is our common heritage. So whether or not you will ever travel in the Holy Land, may this record of our experiences stimulate your interest in the people and the events of the New Testament.

The places associated with the life and work of Christ were revered by Christians already in the New Testament period. The Second Epistle of Peter calls the mount of the Transfiguration "the holy mountain" (1:18), because Jesus sanctified it by his presence. Jewish Christian communities in Palestine preserved the memory of the New Testament sites, and we have records of Christians coming to venerate them well before the Roman empire became officially Christian. Thus, when the Christians of the Constantinian period arrived, they did not need to "discover" these sites, for they had been known and venerated by the uninterrupted presence of Palestinian Christians.

The Byzantines embarked on an enormous construction project, erecting, according to the most recent estimates, more than two hundred churches and monasteries in and around the sacred sites of the Holy Land. The immensity of some of their structures has been revealed by archeological excavations, many of which we visited.

The gospel witness to the faith of the early Christian community cannot be divorced from the time and place in which the events of faith occurred. The gospels are sensitive to the historical circumstances of the time and make numerous references to geography, for the ministry of Christ was public and was conducted in a concrete time and place. When we see the remains of the places where Jesus was born, proclaimed the gospel, died and rose from the dead, we sense the importance of "sacred geography." Visits to these ancient sites, with both their natural settings and archeological excavations, illumine our understanding of the gospel records and the growth of the Church.

In our day some Christian theologians and scholars dismiss the importance of geography and archeological remains. One noted professor turned down several invitations from an archeological society to view the New Testament sites and excavations because he felt that the "truth" of the gospel had to be separated from any reference to particular places and times. And yet what separates Christianity from the ancient mythologies is precisely its historical and geographical concreteness. The professor's attitude was obviously the result of theological presuppositions that regard a great part of the gospel tradition as a fabrication of an anonymous Christian community. This attitude has been subjected to trenchant criticism, particularly by archeologists, whose work is providing other researchers more and more with the "flesh and bone" of the Christian Church.

The places which the New Testament refers to are still there. A great number of them can be positively identified, and many are incorporated into places of worship. In Palestine, the words and events of the gospels are meditated on and relived at the very sites where they occurred. It is not unusual to find pilgrims reading aloud the passages related to the events and places connected with the life of Christ. Veneration throughout the centuries has preserved these places and remains as something more than just monuments of antiquity. In this way, sacred geography and modern archeology also serve to give concrete roots to our faith.

The small territory called the Holy Land, for the most part within the borders of modern Israel, is the homeland of many faiths of the "modern world." As the names Jerusalem, Bethlehem, Capernaum and Mount Carmel resound through the history and literature of all Christian peoples, so they are sacred also to the modern Israeli, the Samaritan, the Arab Muslim and the Druse. Whoever rules in the Holy Land is responsible for many of the world's sacred sites and for the free practice of the expressions of various religious traditions.

It was our good fortune to spend most of our time with Father John Leonard and his wife Barbara, who shared their knowledge with us and inspired us with their enthusiasm. To them and to the Monastery of the Annunciation in Nazareth, which Father John serves, we owe special thanks.

Many others who spoke with us illumined our understanding and helped us to see these monuments in context. We remember them with gratitude. In composing this record, we have drawn not only on our personal experiences but on a number of sources and studies, ancient and modern, dealing with the people and the land. Those most useful to us are listed at the end, and we recommend them to interested readers.

Finally we must thank particularly Professor Georges Barrois, Adjunct Professor of Old Testament at St Vladimir's, who spent many years on the faculty of the Ecole Biblique in Jerusalem before World War II. He showed great interest in our trip, shared with us his intimate and extensive knowledge of the Holy Land and the surrounding areas, and read and commented on our manuscript, as did Fr John Leonard. Any errors of fact or judgment, of course, are ours alone.

We are also grateful to our editors, Paul Kachur and Constance Tarasar, for their sustained interest and useful suggestions, to Theodore Bazil for the preparation of the maps and charts, and to June Magaziner for the excellent illustrations.

Veselin and Lydia W. Kesich

The Sea of Galilee

GALILEE AND SAMARIA

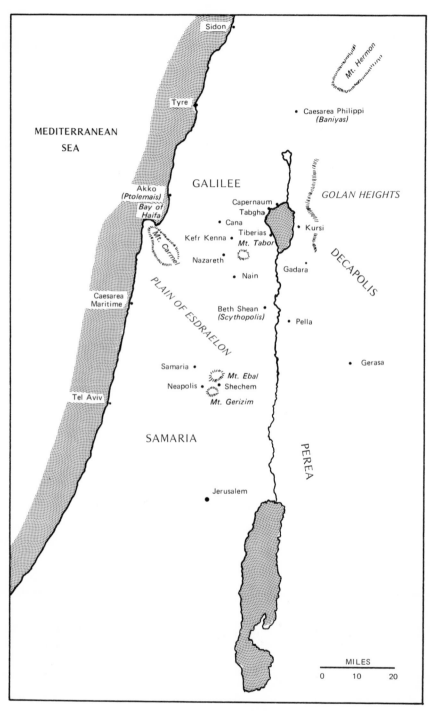

GALILEE AND SAMARIA

Galilee and Its Hellenistic Surroundings

The name Galilee comes from the Hebrew *gelil*, which means region or district. In the eighth century B.C., the prophet Isaiah spoke of the land beyond the Jordan as the "Galilee of the nations," meaning the district of the Gentiles (Isaiah 9:1). Galilee was relatively unimportant in Old Testament history, and not many Israelites settled there after the sixth-century Babylonian captivity. Those who did experienced difficulties living under the heavy pressure of the pagan world. During the period of the Maccabean revolt (168-135 B.C.), the Galilean Jews were brought to Judea, the area of southern Israel around Jerusalem. Only during the reign of John Hyrcanus, around 104 B.C., did they return to the northern province. After the Romans under Pompey captured Jerusalem in 63 B.C., they gradually extended their power throughout Palestine, including Galilee. The ruling family of the Maccabees was then replaced by the Herodians, who were under Roman control. The best known of them is Herod the Great (37-4 B.C.), who became the master of all Palestine.

Herod was a crafty politician who knew how to please the Roman emperor. By culture he belonged to Hellenism, by position he was a Roman viceroy, and by origin he was only very tenuously and dubiously part Jewish, although he was the king of the Jews. He was also evidently a great builder. Among the best known structures he erected were the royal palaces on Herodium and Masada and in Jerusalem. He also rebuilt the cities of Samaria and Caesarea Maritime, and started work on the restoration of the Temple in Jerusalem.

Galilee under Herod the Great and his son Herod Antipas (4 B.C.-39 A.D.) was encircled by Roman power and Hellenistic cities: Caesarea and Akko on the west, the Decapolis to the east and south, and Caesarea Philippi in the north. The region was known for well-constructed and maintained roads in the Roman period. Traffic from the west moved easily to the east, as well as to the north and south. This made Galilee a crossroads and meeting place of different cultures; the homeland of Jesus, in this time, was not at all cut off from the rest of the world.

Our primary authority for first-century geography and the political and religious history of Palestine is the Jewish historian Josephus, who wrote in Rome after the Jewish War of A.D. 66-70. Galilee, he writes, is everywhere fruitful and its soil is "universally rich," and no parts of it lie idle. This is also true today. It is enough to look at the Esdraelon valley from one of Nazareth's hills or from the top of Mount Tabor to see the richness and fertility of the gentle hills surrounding the New Testament sites of Nazareth, Cana and Nain.

Looking down on the Plain of Esdraelon, the visitor sees fields cultivated and irrigated with retaining ponds to equalize the rainwater supply. The fields are now almost entirely farmed by kibbutzim, farming collectives. Many of them have been there for over fifty years. No one owns title to this land, which is leased from the state for definite periods. The kibbutz council allots benefits to the farmers in accordance with its prosperity and their needs; there are no wages or private ownership. As the generations grow and change, conflicts and strains may arise and the original ideology is hard to pass on. Still, the kibbutzim, at least from the outside, give the appearance of prosperity and solidity.

Mt. Carmel and Caesarea Maritime

On the way to Caesarea on the Mediterranean seacoast, the traveler comes to Mount Carmel, or Kérém-El. The "El" is one of the ancient pre-Hebraic terms for "god." Mount Carmel has been regarded as a sacred place at least since the time of the Phoenicians. An Egyptian text of the fifteenth century B.C. calls it the "Holy Headland." The road leads up el-Mukhraka, a peak overlooking the fertile Esdraelon valley on one side and the Bay of Haifa on the other. This peak is also a traditional place of sacrifice. At el-Mukhraka the statue of Elijah—whose very name means "Yahweh is God"—commemorates his triumph there over the worshipers of Baal (1 Kings 18). Near the statue is a small Carmelite monastery, built in 1767. Muslims, Christians and Druse hold annual celebrations here on the feast of Elijah.

To the south of Mount Carmel and el-Mukhraka is Caesarea Maritime, the Roman capital of Palestine and later an important center of Christian mission. The city was primarily the creation of Herod. In 30 B.C., Emperor Augustus gave the fortified town to his vassal king, who named it Caesarea and set about rebuilding it. Here Herod concentrated on essentials: a vast expansion of the harbor with enormous stones protecting it, and impressive aqueducts along the northern shore to guarantee an abundant water supply. Herod's Caesarea witnesses to the fact that the period in which Jesus lived was one of rapid urbanization, complex stirring and mixing of populations, economic and political change and clashing and merging of religious and cultural trends.

Two statues marked the indisputable allegiance of this city to paganism and its culture. The statues, dedicated to Augustus and to Rome, were placed in dominating positions, so that anyone coming to the city by sea or land could easily see them. St Peter could not have missed these pagan monuments when he delivered his famous sermon after baptizing the Roman centurion Cornelius here. "Truly I perceive that God shows no partiality, but in every nation any one who fears him and does what is right is acceptable to him" (Acts 10:34).

Peter's speech is comparable to and no less significant in its theological impact than the sermon St Paul delivered in Athens (Acts 17). And just as the Caesarean statues formed an indispensable background for Peter's speech, the Acropolis provided the context and inspiration for Paul's. Standing in the Areopagus, where pagan philosophers gathered, and looking at the Acropolis, the center of Greek paganism, Paul proclaimed that God "made from one every nation of men to live on all the face of the earth ... that they should seek God, in the hope that they might feel after him and find him. Yet he is not far from each of us, for 'in him we live and move and have our being.'" These are two classic proclamations of the gospel to the Gentiles. Peter spoke in Caesarea Maritime, the Herodian city and the Roman center of power in Palestine, and Paul in Athens, the philosophic center of the ancient world.

St Paul was also in Caesarea. When his life was in danger in Jerusalem, to which he had returned after his conversion, some "brethren" brought him down to Caesarea and from there sent him off to his native city, Tarsus (Acts 9:26ff). During his missionary journeys Paul embarked and disembarked at Caesarea, and he concluded his third missionary journey there, staying in the house of Philip the evangelist (Acts 21: 7-8). This time the people begged him not to go to Jerusalem, but when he decided to go, some disciples from Caesarea went with him. Soon he was to be brought back to Caesarea and spend a full two years (A.D. 58-60) as a prisoner in this city on the Mediterranean coast.

About two hundred years later, still before Christianity became the official religion of the Roman empire, a Christian school was founded in Caesarea. Its head was Origen, the third century biblical scholar, Christian apologist and theologian. He spent about twenty years, from 231 to 250, preaching and teaching here. Later, around 315, the Christian historian Eusebius, who tried to identify the biblical sites in Palestine, would become the bishop of Caesarea.

The most impressive relic of this city today is the completely restored Herodian theater, where modern concertgoers look directly over the stage to the Mediterranean. From the back seats of the theater one has a symbolic view of the history of the town. First there stands Herod's first-century B.C. theater, then the ruins of defensive walls erected by the Byzantine emperor Justinian in the sixth century, and then a row of barbed wire, probably placed

13

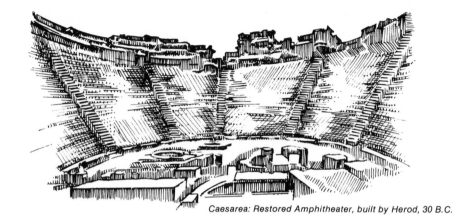

Caesarea: Restored Amphitheater, built by Herod, 30 B.C.

there by the British after World War II to keep Jewish immigrants out, and now maintained by the Israelis to deter Palestinians arriving by sea.

In the courtyard of the theater is a copy of an ancient inscription found there, mentioning Pontius Pilate, the Roman prefect of Judea. There is also a small statue of a shepherd with a lamb over his shoulders. Supposedly, this is a Christian statue, perhaps connected with Origen's university. Some ruins to the left of the road have been tentatively identified with Origen's university and library.

The most prominent ruins, in the center of the town, are the remains of a Crusader citadel, which now houses a restaurant and tourist shops. In the thirteenth century, under the leadership of Louis IX of France, the Crusaders rebuilt only a part of Herod's port, giving their prime attention to this walled and moated sea castle. Louis may have been a saint, but he was also one of the most inept generals in this part of the world, and his citadel was easily taken in 1265 by the Egyptian Mamluks, who leveled the city. The site remained uninhabited from then until 1878, when the Turkish sultan gave it to Muslim refugees from Bosnia (now part of Yugoslavia), whose homeland had come under the control of the Austro-Hungarian empire. The village they built was destroyed in 1948 with the establishment of the Israeli state, leaving intact only a small, attractive mosque.

The Roman procurator had his headquarters (*praetorium*) in Caesarea from 6 A.D. to the fall of Jerusalem in 70, the period embracing the public ministry of Christ and the formative period of the church. It was from here that Pontius Pilate, the Roman procurator, moved to Jerusalem during the Passion

Week. At the time of Jewish feasts and celebrations, the Roman governor with his military power would move from Caesarea up to Jerusalem to keep peace and prevent the rise of anti-Roman militant movements. The procurator would stay in the royal palace, which would become his headquarters, his *praetorium*.

Akko

North of Caesarea Maritime is the ancient harbor of Akko, or Acre. An ancient Canaanite city, it was renamed Ptolemais in 261 B.C. when it came under the control of the Ptolemies of Egypt, one of the families that divided Alexander the Great's empire after his death. St Paul visited Ptolemais at the conclusion of his third missionary journey. A Christian community was already there to receive him, and he stayed there a day before going on to Caesarea (Acts 21:7).

The Arabs conquered the city in 636. In 1104, the Crusaders arrived and replaced them, changing the name of the city again to Saint-Jean-d'Acre. Acre served as the chief port of the Crusaders, and they built a fortress to defend it. Yet in 1187 the city surrendered to Saladin without resistance. One can still see the walls that were built by the Crusaders and refortified by the Albanians under the Ottoman empire in the early nineteenth century. It was in this port also that St Francis of Assisi landed and laid the foundation for the Franciscan custody of many holy sites in Palestine.

The Melchite Church of St Andrew in the Arab section of the town is very little known, but it is prized by connoisseurs because it still retains an eighteenth-century iconostasis with Palestinian-style icons—almost full face, rather heavy set and very much of "this world." In modern times, the memory of any indigenous, individual form of Christianity has been virtually obliterated. The best efforts of outsiders, both Western and Eastern Christians alike, have been directed toward imposing their own forms of Christian expression on local churches rather than encouraging Arab Christians to rediscover their rich heritage.

The Decapolis

Caesarea and Akko were important Hellenistic centers at the time of Christ, linked by good Roman roads with the cities on the Sea of Galilee as well as with the cities of the Decapolis in the east. The Decapolis, a league of ten Hellenistic cities and their territories, served as a buffer zone between Roman power and the indigenous population, and at the same time was a vehicle for

*Roman columns in Gerasa,
a city of the Decapolis.*

spreading Hellenistic culture in this part of the world. The ten cities were brought together into a loose confederation in 63 B.C. by Pompey. Their population was predominantly Gentile, but Jewish communities were also tolerated in them.

The Decapolis is mentioned in the Gospels of Matthew and Mark. Great crowds from the Decapolis listened to the preaching of Jesus (Matthew 4:25), and Jesus himself went through the area healing people (Mark 5:1-20, 7:31). In New Testament times, the most prominent cities of the Decapolis were Gerasa and Gadara, which exercised a strong influence on their regions. Pella, in the Jordan valley, served as a refuge for Christians during the bloody Roman-Jewish struggles of the first century.

Only one of these ten Hellenistic cities, Beth Shean or Scythopolis, was located to the west of the Jordan River. The Romans particularly intended that this city would increase their influence and power in Galilee. The Roman theater there, built in A.D. 200, is one of the best preserved monuments in modern Israel. Beth Shean is an archeologist's dream, with recorded settlements dating back to 3000 B.C.

Beth Shean was mentioned in the Old Testament, in an account at the end of 1 Samuel of the death of Saul, the first king of ancient Israel. The Philistines had defeated the Israelites on Mount Gilboa and had killed Saul's sons. Although Saul himself was wounded rather badly, he had enough strength to fall upon his sword and finish his own life, lest "these uncircumcized come and thrust me through and make sport of me." After the victors found his body, they cut off his head and hung his remains on the walls of Beth Shean.

The city was renamed Scythopolis in the third century B.C. There is a theory that a military colony of Scythian soldiers settled there. From the time of the Maccabees, the Jewish and Gentile communities continued to live peaceably beside each other. In the Byzantine period, Scythopolis became a Christian center and was the home of the well-known Christian historian Cyril of Scythopolis. Cyril is the talented author of the lives of seven Palestinian religious leaders, including Sts Euthymius and Saba. He was himself a disciple of St Saba and entered his monastery.

Caesarea Philippi

To the northeast of Galilee and the Decapolis, under the slope of Mount Hermon, was another Hellenized city, known in New Testament times as Caesarea Philippi and today as Baniyas. Part of Syria before the 1967 war, it is now in Israeli-occupied territory.

From the early third century B.C. this wild and hilly place became a center of the cult of the Greek god Pan. Baniyas is an Arabic form of the Greek name for the city, Panion. When Herod the Great became master of Palestine, he also built a temple to Augustus here. His son Philip rebuilt and expanded the city and renamed it "Caesarea"—after the emperor, adding the designation "Philippi"—after himself, to distinguish it from the coastal city of Caesarea.

Jesus visited the district of Caesarea Philippi with his disciples, although it does not seem that he entered the largely pagan and Gentile city itself. In that region occurred one of the most significant scenes in the gospels:

> **Now when Jesus came into the district of Caesarea Philippi, he asked his disciples, "Who do men say that the Son of man is?" And they said, "Some say John the Baptist, others say Elijah, and others Jeremiah or one of the prophets." He said to them, "But who do you say that I am?" Simon Peter replied, "You are the Christ, the Son of the living God." And Jesus answered him, "Blessed are you, Simon Bar-Jona! For flesh and blood has not revealed this to you, but my Father who is in heaven. And I tell you, you are Peter, and on this rock I will build my church, and the powers of death shall not prevail against it."** *(Matthew 16:13-18)*

Throughout the centuries, Christian interpreters and theologians have probed the meaning of this confession. The geographical context of the exchange can shed some light on its interpretation. Jesus did not ask these questions of his disciples in an isolated village, but beside the great city where the nature god Pan and the human Caesar of Rome were worshiped. Earlier we noted how St Paul delivered a famous sermon against the background of the Acropolis and how Peter spoke under the Roman statues at Caesarea Maritime. Peter's confession at Caesarea Philippi was a proclamation that Jesus is master both of nature and of man, of Pan and the emperor. The setting of the confession is crucial for its interpretation. It is also possible that Jesus called Peter a "rock" (Matthew 16:18), in part, under the impact of the rocky cliffs above the city. In Aramaic, the language which Jesus spoke, *kepha* (Cephas) is both a proper name and the word for "rock." "You are Kepha (Peter), and on this *kepha* (rock) I will build my church."

Once again the city became known to the outside world in medieval times, when the region came under the control of a fanatical sect called *hashshashin*, after their practice of using large amounts of hashish. According to a popular belief, our modern word "assassin" comes from the name of this sect, whose chief object was to assassinate Crusaders. The group was destroyed by the Mongols in the thirteenth century.

Today Baniyas is important for Muslims, Druse and Christians. Here one can see the grotto where the god Pan was worshiped, and on a cliff above it the place where Caesar's statue was erected. There is also a tomb or shrine of the Muslin saint el-Khader or el-Khidr, who bore some of the characteristics of Elijah and St George. One of the sources of the Jordan River lies just under the grotto.

The Sea of Galilee

Outside of Nazareth, about three miles to the northeast, is the city of Kefr Kenna. Many tourists visit this site because it is popularly identified with Cana in Galilee, where Jesus attended a marriage celebration with his disciples and his mother and changed the water into wine (John 2). Many scholars, however, dispute this identification, favoring another place, Khirbert Qana, about nine miles north of Nazareth.

The road from Kefr Kenna leads "down" toward Tiberias. Anyone who travels to any place on the Sea of Galilee is going down, descending. St. Luke records that Jesus "went down to Capernaum" (4:31), for the city is 686 feet below sea level.

The Sea of Galilee, which is referred to twice in the Gospel of John (6:1, 21:1) as the "Sea of Tiberias," is filled with sweet water and many kinds of fish. Josephus wrote that "its waters are sweet, and very agreeable for drinking." It was also, he tells us, "pure, and on every side ends directly at the shores, and at the sand." A nineteenth-century visitor to this region, George Adam Smith, wrote that "the lake of Galilee is at once food, drink, and air, a rest to the eye, coolness in the heat, and escape from the crowd." What the lake was in the past, it still is today.

To the southwest of Tiberias, on the shore of the lake, lies Hammat Tiberias, a complex of ancient buildings that have been excavated and labeled. Most noteworthy is the fourth-century synagogue, whose floor contains a zodiac mosaic. Like Christian art in the same period, it was dependent upon pagan models. The circular central pattern is still clearly visible, although a wall for a later synagogue built over it bisects the pattern. In the center of the circle is Sol Invictus or Helios, the sun god, in his chariot. Around him are the twelve signs of the Zodiac, and in the corners four women depicting the seasons. Images of fruits and birds, as well as menorahs, the Ark of the Law and other Judaic symbols, complete the mosaic. The Mosaic prohibition against images was clearly not in effect here. Another more stylized sixth-century zodiac mosaic floor is in the synagogue at Bet Alpha, at the foot of Mount Gilboa. Both synagogues attest to the number and relative prosperity of the resident Jewish population, a continuing presence in Galilee virtually throughout history. They also show the extent to which the Jewish community participated in the larger culture of the Hellenistic world.

Kursi

The Sea of Galilee is about thirteen miles long and at its widest point eight miles wide. When we first reached the lake it was calm, but soon we noticed a sudden disturbance or storm, which appeared without warning, just as is described in the gospel accounts:

> **And when he got into the boat, his disciples followed him. And behold, there arose a great storm on the sea, so that the boat was being swamped by the waves; but he was asleep. And they went and woke him, saying, "Save, Lord; we are perishing." And he said to them, "Why are you afraid, O men of little faith?" Then he rose and rebuked the winds and the sea; and there was a great calm.**
>
> *(Matthew 8:23-26)*

Continuing north along the eastern shore of the Sea of Galilee, just beyond En Gev, in the area of the Golan Heights, the road crosses what had been the border of Syria before the 1967 war. Here Kursi, the largest monastic complex in Palestine, was discovered only in 1970, when the Israelis started building a road up to the Golan Heights. A large, three-aisled basilica dating from the fifth century is the best preserved of the structures. Byzantine crosses are carved on pillars and stones, and mosaics cover the floor. In the side aisles are pictures of animals, flowers and fruit, which have been systematically defaced.

Kursi's proximity to the lake, together with its hill and cliff, fit well the scene of the gospel story of the healing of the Gerasene demoniac. Jesus delivered him from unclean spirits, whose name was "legion" because there were many of them. After Jesus cast them out of the man, they entered "a great herd of swine (that) was feeding there on the hillside," and the herd "rushed down the steep bank into the sea, and were drowned in the sea" (Mark 5:11-13). The story portrays Jesus in foreign, pagan territory. But the place cannot be Gerasa, a city of the Decapolis thirty-three miles southeast of the lake, for the gospel narrative indicates that the event occurred right on the lake. Therefore, ancient authorities offered variant readings in the text, such as Gadarene and Gergesene. Gadara was another city of the Decapolis located six miles southeast of the Sea of Galilee. Gergesene is possible derived from Gergesa, which may have been Kursi. Thus, it is possible that the Byzantine monastery was built in the area traditionally remembered as the site of the miracle.

After the conversion of Constantine in 313, the attention of the Roman empire shifted to the Holy Land. Numerous rich churches, pilgrimage centers and universities were established by the Byzantines, and for over two hundred years the region knew its greatest stability and prosperity. In the seventh century the Persians, not yet Muslim, swept through, destroying and murdering. This was the first of the destructive waves that buried the Byzantine past, much of which we are only now coming to appreciate. It is hoped that further excavations in the area of the Golan Heights—the high plateau spreading from the Yarmuk River on the south to Mount Hermon in the north—will uncover additional data and throw more light on Byzantine sites in this part of the Middle East. According to some accounts, there were no less than ninety Byzantine sites in the Golan Heights before Omar with his Arab army defeated the Byzantine military in a decisive battle in 638 at the Yarmuk River.

Capernaum

Capernaum, the center of Christ's Galilean ministry, lies on the northwest shore of the Sea of Galilee. In Jesus' time, there were nine cities around the sea, each one numbering ten to fifteen thousand inhabitants. This made it a highly populated area for that time. Capernaum was considerably larger than Christ's native Nazareth. After he was rejected in Nazareth, he could have retreated to another small village, but instead he chose Capernaum and the lake area, where he could reach a wider audience.

Capernaum, whose Hebrew name Kefar-nahum means "village of Nahum" —possibly pointing to the person who originally owned the land—was a busy and prosperous town with a highly profitable fishing industry. Thus, those fishermen who accepted the call of Jesus left a trade that supported themselves and their families rather comfortably to embark on a road to an unknown country. Upon their conversion, they abandoned all that they had to follow the Lord.

The group of determined, hard-working men around Jesus, however, was not confined exclusively to Galilean fishermen. Capernaum was a trade station, with the good Galilean roads facilitating links with cities on the Mediterranean coast as well as the cities of the Decapolis, Damascus and Caesarea Philippi. Here in the neighborhood of Capernaum even people from "the seacoast of Tyre and Sidon came to hear [Jesus] and to be healed of their diseases" (Luke 6:17). A border town, it had a customs house where Levi the son of Alphaeus was sitting one day. When Jesus passed by there, he called out: "Follow me." And Levi, who is usually identified with the apostle Matthew, rose and followed Christ (Mark 2:14).

The world of the first-century Galilean Jews and the world of the Hellenized cities met head-on in Capernaum. Because of these contacts, all Jews of Galilee were looked upon with contempt by Jews of Judea, who considered themselves "pure." When the followers of Jesus came into contact with people from the Decapolis, it may be expected that they communicated with them in Greek.

Greek was the lingua franca at the time of Christ. It was not only the educated who spoke Greek, but also people of the lower classes, many of whom would be characterized as "unlettered." Of course, Aramaic remained the spoken language of the great majority of the people of Galilee. Even in the fourth century, as the pilgrim Egeria and St Jerome witness, the Palestinian churches used both Greek and Aramaic.

Capernaum remained an important Jewish commercial and fishing town in the early Christian centuries. It also became a center of Jewish Christianity. The Jewish Christians there must have been rather numerous, for their existence brought down on them and their city the curse of a famous third-century rabbi, Issil of Caesarea Maritime, who regarded Capernaum as a stronghold of *minim*—that is, "heretics," or Jewish Christians. Both the excavations and data from rabbinic literature indicate that Jews and Jewish Christians lived side by side there. However, although they both had regular contact with people from the Hellenistic cities, it seems they held apart from them, for Capernaum did not have Gentile or Samaritan residents.

With the Arab conquest of Palestine in the seventh century the development of Capernaum seems to have been arrested. We have no indications of the town's existence in the succeeding centuries. A thirteenth-century visitor to Capernaum recorded that "The once renowned town of Capernaum is at present just despicable; it numbers only seven houses of poor fishermen." Today there is no settlement there—only a Franciscan monastery and a Greek Orthodox church to the east of the excavated remains. The excavations of this significant site, begun in 1894 after its purchase by Franciscans from the Bedouin owners, are well kept, marked and under their custody.

To understand the importance of archeological discoveries, the visitor should examine the excavation of Peter's house. As the Gospel records, Jesus visited Peter at his house. After leaving the synagogue, he

entered the house of Simon and Andrew, with James and John. Now Simon's mother-in-law lay sick with a fever, and immediately they told him of her. And he came and took her by the hand and lifted her up, and the fever left her; and she served them.

(Mark 1:29-31)

The house of Peter in Capernaum was an important gathering place for Jewish Christians, who would recall there the events later recorded in the gospels and, it seems, transmit the memory of the sites of Christ's ministry from one generation to another.

Beneath the octagonal Byzantine church erected on this traditional site in the fifth century, archeological excavations have uncovered the remains of a rather small house. In the fourth century, Egeria reports that she was shown the dwelling of the apostle, which had been made into a "house church"—a *domus ecclesia*. After the later construction the house was no longer visible, but the tradition persisted throughout the centuries that the house underneath was Peter's. The modern excavations have given tangible support to this view. The walls of the first-century house remain to the present day, for those who built the octagonal church did not begin by leveling the ground but instead preserved something of the original house and protected it within the church.

Thus, here in Capernaum we have evidence of how the simple house of a fisherman was enlarged to serve as a gathering place for the *minim,* and then became the site of a large, octagonal church with an ornate peacock mosaic floor. The motive behind the transformation of this particular site was the very special regard that Christians held for the house of Peter from the first century on. On the plastered walls of the house, graffiti has been discovered that dates from the period before the Byzantine church was built. Of some 130 items, "Lord Jesus Christ" and "Peter" are the most prominent. These graffiti also testify to the faith in Christ and the high esteem for Peter among Christian residents and pilgrims in Capernaum.

The excavations at Capernaum have also uncovered the remains of a rather imposing synagogue. We know that the Jewish community at the time of

Capernaum: 4th century Synagogue, partially restored.

Jesus had a synagogue in Capernaum—the Gospels testify that Jesus taught in this synagogue and cured a man possessed by an unclean spirit (Mark 1:21-28). All traces of this first-century synagogue, however, seem to have disappeared. The ruins we see today have been decisively dated to the late fourth or early fifth century, on the basis of coins and potsherds found imbedded in layers of mortar. This large structure is considered to have been one of the most splendid synagogues ever found in Palestine. The Roman versions of Greek pillars and the sophisticated and elegant construction reflect the same post-Alexandrian Hellenistic world that we had seen in Philippi in Greece. The house of meeting was built upon a raised platform, to accord with the Jewish prescription that the synagogue must be higher than any house for ordinary use around it. There is an old saying: "Any town whose roofs are higher than the synagogue will end in destruction." Private houses that have been excavated in Capernaum are indeed very small, low and poor compared to the excavated synagogue.

Beneath the ruins of the large synagogue of the fourth or fifth century, house foundations from an earlier century have been discovered. This may provide us with a clue to the location of Capernaum's first-century Jewish house of meeting. Although we may never be sure as to its exact site, we cannot exclude the possibility that the synagogue that Jesus taught in was originally a house which was enlarged or modified to serve the needs of a house of prayer, and the magnificent Byzantine-era structure may have been built over this first-century place of worship. This would parallel the development of the octagonal Byzantine church, built on the site of the house-church in which Peter had lived. Still, it remains a mystery why the Capernaum Jews of the Byzantine period would erect their large and splendid synagogue only a few yards away from the site of Peter's house and the octagonal Byzantine church.

We have already mentioned that remains of private houses have also been excavated in Capernaum. Some of these date to the first century, and feature an outside stairway leading up to a flat roof constructed of beams and clay mixed with straw. These light, flat tops were used for sleeping during the hot summer months, for drying vegetables or for a place of withdrawal for prayer. The structure of these houses gives us a better understanding of the narrative of the healing of the paralytic given by St Mark (2:1-12). When the people of Capernaum heard that Jesus had returned to their city from Galilee, many gathered together at the house where he was preaching. Then four men brought a paralytic to the house to be healed by Jesus. "And when they could not get near him because of the crowd, they removed the roof above him; and when they made an opening, they let down the pallet on which the paralytic lay." The outside steps gave easy access to the roof, which could easily be removed and repaired. St Luke reports the same miraculous healing of the paralytic, but he does not seem to have in mind the Palestinian houses of Jesus' time, referring to a tiled roof of, apparently, a Greco-Roman house.

> **On one of those days, as he was teaching, there were Pharisees and teachers of the law sitting by, who had come from every village of Galilee and Judea and from Jerusalem; and the power of the Lord was with him to heal. And behold, men were bringing on a bed a man who was paralyzed, and they sought to bring him in and lay him before Jesus; but finding no way to bring him in, because of the crowd, they went up on the roof and let him down with his bed through the tiles in the midst before Jesus.** *(Luke 5:17-19)*

It is difficult to imagine how a man could be let down through such a tiled roof.

Tabgha

A short distance from Capernaum lies Tabgha, a rocky area with a solitary view of the hills near the Sea of Galilee. The name of this place comes from the Greek Heptapegon, which means "place of seven springs." There is no archeological evidence of any settlements here in New Testament times, but in the fourth century it was the site of churches marking the Sermon on the Mount, the multiplication of the loaves and fishes, and the post-resurrection appearance on the lake.

The Church of the Multiplication is the most impressive structure at Tabgha. The feeding of the multitude, the only miracle that appears in all four gospels, is supposed to have occurred here. The gospel account indicates that it took place not far from the lake, in an isolated, lonely place. After hearing of the death of John the Baptist, Jesus

> **withdrew from there in a boat to a lonely place apart. But when the crowds heard it, they followed him on foot from the towns. As he went ashore he saw a great throng; and he had compassion on them, and healed their sick. When it was evening, the disciples came to him and said, "This is a lonely place, and the day is now over; send the crowds away to go into the villages and buy food for themselves." Jesus said, "They need not go away; you give them something to eat." They said to him, "We have only five loaves here and two fish." And he said, "Bring them here to me." Then he ordered the crowds to sit down on the grass; and taking the five loaves and the two fish he looked up to heaven, and blessed, and**

Tabgha: 5th century mosaic of loaves and fishes, Church of the Multiplication

broke and gave the loaves to the disciples, and the disciples gave them to the crowds. And they all ate and were satisfied. And they took up twelve baskets full of the broken pieces left over. And those who ate were about five thousand men, besides women and children. *(Matthew 14:13-21)*

The fourth-century mosaic floor of the church, called by J. Murphy-O'Connor "the most beautiful mosaic floor in the country," displays birds, animals and plants in exquisite and graceful patterns.

The site of the appearance of Christ to his disciples after his resurrection is marked on the lake shore. Over the still visible remains of a larger fourth-century church there stands the modern Catholic Church of the Primacy, built in 1933. In front of its altar is a large, flat rock, called the *mensa domini* (table of the Lord), which is revered as the place on which the risen Christ placed the bread when he prepared the meal for his disciples:

After this Jesus revealed himself again to the disciples by the Sea of Tiberias; and he revealed himself in this way. Simon Peter, Thomas called the Twin, Nathanael of Cana in Galilee, the sons of Zebedee, and two others of his disciples were together. Simon Peter said to them, "I am going fishing." They said to him, "We will go with you." They went out and got into the boat; but that night they caught nothing.

Just as day was breaking, Jesus stood on the beach; yet the disciples did not know that it was Jesus. Jesus said to them, "Children,

have you any fish?" They answered him, "No." He said to them, "Cast the net on the right side of the boat, and you will find some." So they cast it, and now they were not able to haul it in, for the quantity of fish. That disciple whom Jesus loved said to Peter, "It is the Lord!" When Simon Peter heard that it was the Lord, he put on his clothes for he was stripped for work, and sprang into the sea. But the other disciples came in the boat, dragging the net full of fish, for they were not far from the land, but about a hundred yards off.

When they got out on land, they saw a charcoal fire there, with fish lying on it, and bread. Jesus said to them, "Bring some of the fish that you have just caught." So Simon Peter went aboard and hauled the net ashore, full of large fish, a hundred and fifty-three of them; and although there were so many, the net was not torn. Jesus said to them, "Come and have breakfast." Now none of the disciples dared ask him, "Who are you?" They knew it was the Lord. Jesus came and took the bread and gave it to them, and so with the fish. This was now the third time that Jesus was revealed to the disciples after he was raised from the dead.　　　　　　*(John 21:1-14)*

According to John, this was Christ's third post-resurrection appearance.

When they had finished breakfast, Jesus said to Simon Peter, "Simon, son of John, do you love me more than these?" He said to him, "Yes, Lord; you know that I love you." He said to him, "Feed my lambs." A second time he said to him, "Simon, son of John, do you love me?" He said to him, "Yes, Lord; you know that I love you." He said to him, "Tend my sheep." He said to him the third time, "Simon, son of John, do you love me?" Peter was grieved because he said to him the third time, "Do you love me?" And he said to him, "Lord, you know everything; you know that I love you." Jesus said to him, "Feed my sheep. . . ."　　　　　　*(John 21:15-17)*

The Roman Catholic Church sees this dialogue as proof of Peter's primacy. The early Christian Church, on the other hand, interpreted it as the restoration of Peter to the full status of Christ's disciple and apostle. Peter had denied Christ three times before his death and resurrection; now, Christ's threefold question demanded from Peter a threefold expression of allegiance in love.

Nearby this church is a hill with several caves, which is regarded as the location of the Sermon on the Mount. Little remains of the fourth-century church that had been built there. On what is now called the Mount of the Beatitudes, an octagonal Roman Catholic church, built in 1938, commands a beautiful view over the Sea of Galilee.

Tiberias

Tiberias, the chief city on the Sea of Galilee, had been built by Herod Antipas around A.D. 13 and was dedicated to the Roman emperor Tiberius. Although Jesus proclaimed the gospel to the people living around the lake and visited many of its surrounding cities and villages, it appears that he avoided the city of Tiberias itself. The usual explanation for this has been that he wished to avoid arrest before his hour had come. We should also note, however, that pious Galilean Jews of the time shunned Herod Antipas' place of residence because they believed that in the process of building the city he had desecrated ancient tombs.

Because of the presence and work of Jesus Christ on the Sea of Galilee, these places belong to the "spiritual geography" of the entire Christian world. Here one sees pilgrimage sites and Byzantine structures, all in the startlingly beautiful, unspoiled setting of the lake. This physical setting, so well preserved, helps to make the events of two thousand years ago concrete and immediate.

Nazareth

Nazareth today is not one but two separate cities. Arab Nazareth, containing the ancient Christian sites, is centered in the valley. About 40,000 people now live there. On a steep slope above it is situated new Nazareth, the Jewish city, which is quite cut off from the Arab town. Upper Nazareth, which has been completely reconstructed since 1970, is the home for some twenty thousand people, and according to plan is to grow until its population exceeds that of lower Nazareth. However, the Arab population is continuing to grow as well, as people move from the country to the town.

In the time of Jesus, Nazareth was a small village, probably with only about four or five hundred inhabitants—although some estimates are higher. The villagers were engaged primarily in agriculture and were rather poor, as archeological excavations confirm. Although Nazareth was close to important trade routes, the population remained exclusively Jewish. For this reason, it was to be one of the towns chosen as the residence of a group of the priests who were forced to leave Jerusalem when the Temple was destroyed in A.D. 70. But in the time of Jesus, even the residents of the neighboring villages considered Nazareth insignificant. When Philip asserted that "We have found him of whom Moses in the law and also the prophets wrote, Jesus of Nazareth, the son of Joseph," Nathaniel, from nearby Cana, responded: "Can anything good come out of Nazareth?" (John 1:45-46).

Lower Nazareth

29

The gospels record that Mary and Joseph lived in Nazareth. There is a question, however, among biblical researchers as to whether they lived here before the birth of the Messiah. The Gospel of Matthew implies that Jesus' family lived in Bethlehem even before his birth, and only later moved to Galilee. According to the Gospel of Luke, Jesus was born after his parents left Nazareth for Bethelehem, the city of David, ninety miles away, to be inscribed on the tax rolls there because Joseph was of the house and lineage of David. They agree nevertheless that after Christ's birth in Bethlehem the holy family did dwell in Nazareth, and Jesus was brought up there. Matthew tells us that Nazareth was his native town, and his mother Mary and his cousins lived there.

If Jesus was Mary's only son, as the Church has always taught, then who were the brothers of Jesus, who are mentioned in all the Gospels as well as in Acts and in St. Paul's Letter to the Galatians: "Then after three years I went up to Jerusalem to visit Cephas, and remained with him fifteen days. But I saw none of the other apostles except James the Lord's brother" (1:18-19). The term "brother" *(adelphos)* in Near Eastern culture may point to various degrees of blood relationship or "step-brother," as well as blood brother in the ordinary sense. In Matthew, for instance, we find:

> **and coming to his own country he taught them in their synagogue,
> so that they were astonished, and said, "Where did this man get this
> wisdom and these mighty works? Is not this the carpenter's son? Is
> not his mother called Mary? And are not his brothers James and
> Joseph and Simon and Judas? And are not all his sisters with us?
> Where then did this man get all this?"** *(Matthew 13:54-56)*

But another passage helps us to see just what is meant by the term "brother":

> **There were also many women there, looking on from afar, who had
> followed Jesus from Galilee, ministering to him; among whom were
> Mary Magdalene, and Mary the mother of James and Joseph and
> the mother of the sons of Zebedee.** *(Matthew 27:55-56)*

Mark also records this distinction (6:30 and 15:40). It would be inconceivable that Matthew and Mark would describe Mary, the mother of Jesus, in such a roundabout way as the "Mother of James and Joseph." James and Joseph might well be the children of Mary, the wife of Clopas, who is mentioned in St. John's account of the crucifixion: "Standing by the cross of Jesus were his mother, and his mother's sister, Mary the wife of Clopas, and Mary Magdalene" (19:25). Hegesippus, the second century writer, identified Clopas as the brother of Joseph. His sons James and Joseph then would be cousins of Jesus, not blood brothers.

Mary was well known in Nazareth. In the earliest of the gospels Jesus was identified not as the son of Joseph, as the custom of the time would require, but as the son of Mary (Mark 6:3). This would indicate that Mary was held in special esteem in Nazareth. Graffiti has been discovered there, dating from the second and third centuries, praising Mary—one states, in Greek, XE MAPIA, "Rejoice, Mary." This is evidence that the Virgin was venerated by the Jewish Christian community of Nazareth long before the Third Ecumenical Council (431), when dogmatic expression was given to the faith that had started much earlier.

House of Mary

Egeria, a very energetic, intelligent and observant pilgrim from Gaul or Spain (or possibly some other western province of the Roman empire), visited the Holy Land and Nazareth in 384 and reported that she was shown in the native town of Christ "a big and very splendid cave in which Mary had lived." The Christians in the village had been venerating this cave since very early times. At the beginning of the fifth century, Byzantine Christians built a large church over another structure that had been erected sometime before over the "house of Mary." Excavations of this site strongly suggest that the earlier structure was a church erected by the Jewish Christians of Nazareth—a "synagogue church." Thus, a Judeo-Christian church was transformed into a large basilica. The Byzantine basilica lasted until the arrival of the Crusaders in Palestine. The Crusaders, in their turn, built another church at the beginning of the twelfth century, which was then destroyed in 1263. In the seventeenth century, the Franciscans came to Nazareth and purchased the holy ground, and they constructed a rather small church over the "splendid cave" in 1730.

Today we have over the cave an enormous, modern Latin basilica, completed and consecrated in 1969. This modern complex has two levels: a lower church, which contains the cave itself as well as a pre-Byzantine baptistry, and directly above it a more elaborate upper church.

Here it is not unusual to find a pilgrim reading Isaiah 7, which contains the prophecy of the birth of Christ:

> Again the Lord spoke to Ahaz, "Ask a sign of the Lord your God; let it be deep as Sheol or high as heaven." But Ahaz said, "I will not ask, and I will not put the Lord to the test." And he said, "Hear then, O house of David! Is it too little for you to weary men, that you weary

my God also? Therefore the Lord himself will give you a sign. Behold, a virgin shall conceive and bear a son, and shall call his name Immanuel, (God with us). *(Isaiah 7:10-14)*

The cave behind the altar and the remains of previous churches that have existed on this spot give particular meaning to this reading.

In the lower church, behind the altar, one can see the cave of Mary—the Grotto. This treasured excavation, which seems to have been a storage cellar or other subterranean dependency of the "House where Mary lived," is well preserved and was incorporated into the very structure of the church. The walls of the cave appear, even to the non-archeological eye, to be very old and in danger of collapsing if not protected. Archeologists date the walls to the first century A.D. or perhaps even to the century before. Altogether this lower church leaves a most profound impression.

Church of St Gabriel

The most significant event in Mary's life in Nazareth was the Annunciation, told to us by St Luke. The angel Gabriel was sent from God to Nazareth,

to a virgin betrothed to a man whose name was Joseph, of the house of David; and the virgin's name was Mary. And he came to her and said, "Hail, O favored one, the Lord is with you!" But she was greatly troubled at the saying, and considered in her mind what sort of greeting this might be. And the angel said to her, "Do not be afraid, Mary, for you have found favor with God. And behold, you will conceive in your womb and bear a son, and you shall call his name Jesus.

He will be great, and will be called the Son of the
  Most High;
and the Lord God will give to him the throne of his
  father David,
and he will reign over the house of Jacob forever;
and of his kingdom there will be no end."

And Mary said to the angel, "How shall this be, since I have no husband?" And the angel said to her,

"The Holy Spirit will come upon you,
and the power of the Most High will overshadow you;
therefore the child to be born will be called holy,
the Son of God. *(Luke 1:27-35)*

This passage does not identify the location of this event, nor describe the circumstances under which Mary heard the voice, the greeting and the message of salvation brought by the angel Gabriel. The apocryphal text known as the *Protoevangelium of James,* however, is more specific on these points. According to this second-century document, "Mary took the pitcher and went forth to draw water and heard a voice." When she returned to her home, the angel was standing before her and saying, "Do not fear, Mary, for you have found grace before the Lord . . . and shall conceive of his Word."

Echoes of this text are found in Nazareth, in the Greek Orthodox Church of St Gabriel. This church is much smaller than the large Latin basilica of the Annunciation, but it fits its surroundings well. Although newly frescoed and restored, its earlier prosperity and care are no longer apparent. The intricately carved Cretan iconostasis is rotting away and will be difficult to restore. At the entrance to the church, the sound of running water can be heard coming from a well or spring that is incorporated into the structure of the building. The spring, which is located on the left of the church as one faces the altar, feeds the present "Well of Mary," situated about 150 yards outside the church. But the spring inside the church is most probably the place where Mary and the other women of the ancient village used to come to draw water for their homes.

Although this spring is not mentioned in the canonical story of the Annunciation, it should not be dismissed out of hand as unauthentic. The gospels are silent on many details, yet this silence should not be interpreted to mean that details preserved in other ancient traditions are always inaccurate. The spring of Nazareth did exist in the time of Jesus, and it would have been natural for Mary to go regularly to this spring. Even today it fills the silence of the gospels. As the cave of Mary was incorporated into the Church of the Annunciation, similarly the spring of Mary formed part of the Church of St Gabriel. In both cases, the very simple remains of a holy site served as the basis for a church dedicated to the event that took place there.

The Hill of the Precipitation

Close to Arab Nazareth there is a cliff associated with the rejection of Christ in his native town (Luke 4), known as the Hill of the Precipitation. Jesus

came to Nazareth, where he had been brought up; and he went to the synagogue, as the custom was, on the sabbath day. And he stood up to read; and there was given to him the book of the

prophet Isaiah. He opened the book and found the place where it was written,

> "The Spirit of the Lord is upon me,
> because he has anointed me to preach good news to
>   the poor.
> He has sent me to proclaim release to the captives
> and recovering of sight to the blind,
> to set at liberty those who are oppressed,
> to proclaim the acceptable year of the Lord."

And he closed the book, and gave it back to the attendant, and sat down; and the eyes of all in the synagogue were fixed on him. And he began to say to them, "Today this scripture has been fulfilled in your hearing." And all spoke well of him, and wondered at the gracious words which proceeded out of his mouth; and they said, "Is not this Joseph's son?" And he said to them, "Doubtless you will quote to me this proverb, 'Physician, heal yourself; what we have heard you did at Capernaum, do here also in your own country,'" And he said, "Truly, I say to you, no prophet is acceptable in his own country. But in truth, I tell you, there were many widows in Israel in the days of Elijah, when the heaven was shut up three years and six months, when there came a great famine over all the land; and Elijah was sent in the land of Sidon, to a woman who was a widow. And there were many lepers in Israel in the time of the prophet Elisha; and none of them was cleansed, but only Naaman the Syrian." When they heard this, all in the synagogue were filled with wrath. And they rose up and put him out of the city, and led him to the brow of the hill on which their city was built, that they might throw him down headlong. But passing through the midst of them he went away.   *(Luke 4:16-30)*

Here Jesus compared himself to the two great prophets of ancient Israel, Elijah and Elisha. As they had done in their own time, so Jesus in his day would lead his disciples beyond the confines of the established religion, customs and tradition and out to the world beyond, to help and heal the Gentiles. Jesus reminded the people of Nazareth that Elijah was not sent to anyone in Israel in the time of drought and famine, but to a widow in the land of Sidon, Zarephath. Elijah saved the woman and her household, and brought her son, in whom there was no breath left, back to life. "Now I know that you are a man of God, and that the word of the Lord in your mouth is truth," said the woman to Elijah (1 Kings 17). She recognized who Elijah was, but the people of Nazareth did not know who Jesus was.

Then Jesus compared his task to the work of Elisha, who was not sent to heal any of the many lepers in Israel but to Naaman, the commander of the army of the king of Syria. Having heeded Elisha's message, Naaman was cured, and he praised the God of Israel (2 Kings 5). But the people of Nazareth rejected the message of Jesus, whom God had sent to them. They even went beyond sheer rejection: they wanted to kill their "prophet," rising up and leading him to the crest of a hill that they might throw him headlong down it.

The present Hill of the Precipitation does not suit the description we find in the Gospel of Luke. The Nazareth of Jesus' time was a small village surrounded by several cliffs from which a person could fall to his death, and Jesus might have been taken to any one of them. But St Luke speaks specifically about the hill "on which their city was built." The present Hill of the Precipitation is located outside the expanded modern city of Nazareth and far away from the original village. The hill that Luke had in mind has apparently been absorbed as the town grew. Even today, as you look at the area of the holy places—the house and well of Mary—as well as of the ancient synagogue of Nazareth, you can detect that the houses were built on the sloping side of what had probably been an ancient hill. Still, the modern Hill of the Precipitation, although not an authentic site, is very precipitous and serves as a vivid reminder that Jesus was rejected in his native city.

Mount Tabor

From the heights of Nazareth one is afforded an excellent view of the many rolling hills of Galilee. Mount Tabor, rising 1,300 feet above the plain, is unquestionably the most attractive hill of them all. This traditional site of Christ's Transfiguration, situated between Nazareth and the Sea of Galilee, could never be mistaken for any other because of its round, symmetrical shape.

Approaching Mount Tabor from the western side of the hill, one sees on the right the village of Nain, where Jesus resurrected the only son of a widow.

> **Jesus went to a city called Nain, and his disciples and a great crowd went with him. As he drew near to the gate of the city, behold, a man who had died was being carried out, the only son of his mother, and she was a widow; and a large crowd from the city was with her. And when the Lord saw her, he had compassion on her and said to her, "Do not weep." And he came and touched the bier, and the bearers stood still. And he said, "Young man, I say to you, arise." And the dead man sat up, and began to speak. And he gave him to his**

mother. Fear seized them all; and they glorified God, saying, "A great prophet has arisen among us!" and "God has visited his people!" And this report concerning him spread through the whole of Judea and all the surrounding country. *(Luke 7:11-17)*

Nain, now an Arab Muslim village, is located on a gentle slope, at a distance of about half a mile from the main road.

At the top of Mount Tabor, in a central position, stands the Franciscan Church of the Transfiguration. A modern replica of the Byzantine basilica of Tourmanin in northern Syria, it was constructed in 1924 over an ancient base. Christian churches and settlements had been built on this site at least since the sixth century, and the mount had been a prominent location centuries before that. It is mentioned in the Old Testament: Deborah, a prophetess, Israel's ruler,

> **was judging Israel at that time . . . and the people of Israel came up [into the hill country of Ephraim] to her for judgment. She sent and summoned Barak . . . and said to him, "The Lord, God of Israel, commands you, 'Go, gather your men at Mount Tabor, taking ten thousand from the tribe of Naphtali and the tribe of Zebulun'. . . So Barak went down from Mount Tabor with ten thousand men following him. And the Lord routed Sisera and all his chariots and all his army before Barak at the edge of the sword . . . all the army of Sisera fell by the edge of the sword; not a man was left.**
> *(Judges 4:5-6, 14-16)*

After Sisera and Jabin, the King of Canaan, were routed, Deborah and Barak celebrated the victory by singing, making "melody to the Lord, the God of Israel" (Judges 5:3).

The modern Catholic church is situated inside an abandoned Benedictine monastery. It shows the outline of an older Byzantine church, and is built on two levels. There is an attractive peacock window in the crypt chapel.

The Greek Orthodox Church of St Elijah is not as imposing as the modern Catholic Church, but it still is large enough, with its spacious outdoor courtyard, to accommodate several hundred worshipers for services on the feast of the Transfiguration. The building is a Crusader chapel, and contains a rare Palestinian icon of Jesus dressed as a bishop, seated in a bishop's chair, dating from the eighteenth century.

The event of the Transfiguration greatly impressed Peter and the other disciples. As Mark records:

> **Jesus took with him Peter and James and John, and led them up a high mountain apart by themselves; and he was transfigured before**

Transfiguration of Christ

them, and his garments became glistening, intensely white, as no fuller on earth could bleach them. And there appeared to them Elijah with Moses; and they were talking to Jesus. And Peter said to Jesus, "Master, it is well that we are here; let us make three booths, one for you and one for Moses and one for Elijah." For he did not know what to say, for they were exceedingly afraid. And a cloud overshadowed them, and a voice came out of the cloud, "This is my beloved Son; listen to him." And suddenly looking around they no longer saw any one with them but Jesus only. *(Mark 9:2-8)*

Standing on the top of Mount Tabor, we can easily understand why Peter wanted to stay there. His first reason, of course, was the beauty of the vision of the transfigured Christ with Moses and Elijah. But perhaps he was also inspired by the view from the top of Mount Tabor. Beyond the surrounding fields and hills one can see the Horns of Hattin—a long, low hill to the west of the Sea of Galilee with little peaks at each end—and between the green plain and blue sky to the west look back also on Nazareth.

When Jesus proclaimed the gospel in Galilee, he was announcing the coming of his kingdom not in an obscure, isolated corner but in a region where two distinct worlds came together. Galilee provided Christ with his first

37

dedicated disciples, who followed him to Jerusalem and witnessed his death and resurrection. After his resurrection, Jesus appeared to them at the Sea of Galilee and had a meal with them. Thus, the messianic community, with the Messiah at its head, came into existence in Galilee.

Galilee is encircled on all sides by Hellenistic monuments and ruins. These remains are very important for understanding the Bible and the gospels as a whole. Contemporary archeology is enthusiastically recovering a past that threatened to slip into myth and is continually revealing treasures of art and building that still persist and survive despite war and decay. These remains, the rocks and ruins, throw additional light on the gospel text and help us to grasp its meaning more firmly. The gospel is given in human words, inspired by the spirit, and it is important to include all the data available to us in our effort to understand the narrative.

The richly conflicting history of Galilee contributes to the meaning of the events that occurred there, for the verbal image of the gospel can never be separated from its history and geography, its time and place. We are well accustomed to speaking about sacred history, but we should not forget the link between the events of salvation and the sites where Jesus lived and worked—there is also a "sacred geography." For those who know the words of Christ and their message, every place touched by his presence is also full of color and meaning.

Certain pilgrims and scholars come to Galilee to look for what they assume was primitive Christianity in its pure form. They are interested in the origins of the Christian movement, and they attempt to separate the beginning of the faith from its subsequent development, which they regard as a hindrance to our understanding. But it is enough to examine the archeological remains in Capernaum or Nazareth to recognize the organic link between Christian origins and Christian growth. The modest first-century house in Capernaum that was transformed first into a house church and then into an octagonal Byzantine church, along with its first-century graffiti expressing a high Christology, attests to the true relationship of the two. Christian origins are related to Christian growth as the seed is to the tree. One cannot be examined without the light shed by the other. Those who look for the primitive, "pure Christianity" forget that Christian development belongs to the "spirit of truth," which has guided Christians into all truth (John 16:13). The remains of Capernaum and Nazareth have a great symbolic value for us, and stand as a warning not to separate "Jesus of Nazareth" from the "Christ of faith" or from the Church and its growth in history.

From Nazareth to Jerusalem

Pilgrimage road in Samaria

The Pilgrimage Road

Leaving Nazareth, the city of the Annunciation, we turn now to Jerusalem, the city of the Resurrection. Pilgrimage to Jerusalem was a regular part of Jewish religious life in the time of Jesus. The law demanded that the pilgrimage to Jerusalem be undertaken three times a year, for three major feasts: Passover, Pentecost, and Tabernacles:

> **Three times in the year you shall keep a feast for me. You shall keep the feast of unleavened bread, as I commanded you, you shall eat unleavened bread for seven days at the appointed time in the month of Abib, for in it you came out of Egypt. None shall appear before me empty-handed. You shall keep the feast of harvest, of the first fruits of your labor, of what you sow in the field. You shall keep the feast of ingathering at the end of the year, when you gather in from the field the fruit of your labor. Three times in the year shall all your males appear before the Lord God.** *(Ex. 23:14-17)*

The text reflects the custom of making a pilgrimage to the main sanctuary of the Hebrew tribes at Shiloh, as mentioned in I Samuel 1:3. This is the period before the monarchy was established in Israel. We also find an account of pilgrimage festivals in Deuteronomy 16:16-17, given in summary form. This account, of a later period, places the center of pilgrimage in the Temple in Jerusalem.

The first pilgrimage is on the feast of the unleavened bread, the feast of Passover. The second, the feast of harvest or the feast of weeks, was celebrated at the time of the wheat harvest, fifty days after Passover. Later it was called Pentecost, based on the Greek word for "fifty." The third, the feast of ingathering, or the feast of booths, is celebrated at the end of the year, in autumn.

All these three ancient agricultural feasts were historicized and transformed over the course of Hebrew history. By the time of Jesus, they came to celebrate three crucial events in the Old Testament history of salvation: Passover—the Exodus of the people from slavery in Egypt; Pentecost—the giving of the Law to Moses on Mount Sinai; and the feast of booths or Tabernacles—the sojourn of the Israelites in the wilderness when they lived in tents.

For those who lived far from Jerusalem, such as the Galilean Jews, the requirements that they should make a pilgrimage to Jerusalem were modified so that only a Passover pilgrimage was required. Being brought up in a pious Jewish home in Nazareth, Jesus naturally took part with his family in these pilgrimages. St Luke records in his Gospel that Mary and Joseph "went to Jerusalem every year at the feast of Passover. And when [Jesus] was twelve years old, they went up according to custom" (2:41-42).

Undertaking a pilgrimage from Nazareth to Jerusalem in Jesus' time was not easy. The Jews of Nazareth could not take the shorter road, for it led through ancient Samaria, and there was great hostility between the Jews and the Samaritans. Instead, they were obliged to take a longer route through Perea, on the eastern side of the Jordan River. But although the pilgrims avoided unfriendly Samaria, they could not avoid the pagan city Beth Shean, or Scythopolis—which, as we have already mentioned, was a city of the Decapolis situated on the west of the Jordan River.

In his informative and sensitive book *The Jewish Jesus,* Robert Aron offers a vivid picture and description of the movements of these pilgrims. The journey would take at least four days, which the pilgrims would fill by singing hymns and talking about the coming of the Messiah while walking on toward Jerusalem. The first day would bring them from Nazareth to Beth Shean, which was a flourishing and prosperous town in the first century A.D. "If paradise is to be found in Palestine," wrote an ancient rabbi, "the door to it is Beth Shean." The city was located in a rich and fertile part of Palestine, and was well known for its olives. It also had a Jewish community, which was known for its observance of the law and which was ready to accommodate pilgrims from Nazareth. However, Beth Shean or Scythopolis was also a

Roman city with pagan customs and well-preserved Roman monuments. But with all its prosperity, its inhabitants had little hope of a future life—if we may judge by inscriptions on tombs discovered in that region, which read "After all things a tomb" and "No one is immortal." It is quite possible that the twelve-year-old Jesus, like many others from Nazareth, encountered here for the first time the Roman pagan world, so different in religion and aspirations from the Jewish village of Nazareth.

After spending the night in Beth Shean the pilgrims, full of hope and messianic expectation, would cross the Jordan River and turn south down the steadily sloping valley. From there the valley drops some eight hundred feet to the Dead Sea—at 1,286 feet below sea level, the lowest point of land on earth. Five miles north of the sea they would reach Jericho, an oasis also known for its fruit trees.

The last day of the pilgrimage would be spent climbing from Jericho to Jerusalem, from 820 feet below sea level to 2,700 feet above. The road goes through thirteen miles of the Judean desert. Modern tourists and pilgrims can drive and enjoy the desert scenery, and rejoice when the city on Mount Zion finally appears. We can only imagine what joy the Galilean pilgrims, who traveled on foot, must have felt when, exhausted by the strenuous climb up and up, they raised their heads to see cultivated fields, olives, vineyards and the holy city.

When they reached Bethany, about two miles east of Jerusalem, they would climb the Mount of Olives, with its unforgettable view of the city and the Temple. After finally seeing their goal they would descend to Gethsemane and the valley of the brook Kidron. Then again they would climb, to the mount of the Temple, enter by one of its eastern gates and purify themselves in the pool of Bethzatha.

Today the visitor to Israel cannot follow the pilgrimage road in its entirety, but he can visit many of the sites along the way. He can travel from Nazareth to Beth Shean, and from Jericho to Jerusalem. He can share with these early pilgrims the view of the city from the Mount of Olives and visit the Temple Mount.

Samaria (West Bank) and Nablus

The road that the traveler follows today from Nazareth to Jerusalem may lead along the Mediterranean coast. Our road, however, took us through the West Bank, approximately the territory of ancient Samaria. Even from the hills of Nazareth we could see the heights of Samaria. The distance from Nazareth to Jerusalem on this road is eighty-five miles.

The modern traveler notes along this inland road traces of the Six-Day War of 1967, such as burnt-out tanks. The main city along this route is Nablus, where the overwhelming majority of the population is Arab Muslim. There are also some Arab Christians and several hundred Samaritans.

The location of Nablus has a significant place in biblical history. On the outskirts of town rises the mound of Tell el-Balata, which is the site of ancient Shechem. In Hebrew *shechem* means "shoulder." The site is positioned between the two "shoulders" of Mount Ebal and Mount Gerizim. Shechem was an ancient Canaanite city to which Abram came after receiving the promise and call of God almost four thousand years ago. It was the scene of the first theophany—the Lord's appearance to Abram at the oak of Moreh (Genesis 12:1-7).

Later Shechem became the center of the ancient Israelite tribes. In the twelfth century B.C., Joshua gathered all the tribes at Shechem and made a covenant with them. The last chapter of the book of Joshua, in which this event is recorded, gives us a summary of the history of Israel from the call of Abram up to Joshua's conquest of the promised land.

> **Then Joshua gathered all the tribes of Israel to Shechem, and summoned the elders, the heads, the judges, and the officers of Israel; and they presented themselves before God. And Joshua said to all the people, "Thus says the Lord, the God of Israel, 'Your fathers lived of old beyond the Euphrates, Terah, the father of Abraham and of Nahor; and they served other gods. Then I took your father Abraham from beyond the River and led him through all the land of Canaan, and made his offspring many.** *(Joshua 24:1-3)*

Archeological excavations at Shechem indicate that the city was not destroyed in Joshua's time. This gives us good reason to believe that the movement of the ancient Hebrews into Palestine was not the result of military victories alone but also developed out of a long process of assimilation and integration of other peoples in Palestine. This is supported by evidence from the book of Joshua itself. The covenant that Joshua made with the tribes in Shechem appears to have been a peaceful union of indigenous peoples with the tribes that arrived with Joshua. On the basis of such archeological and literary sources, many researchers have concluded that not all of the ancient Hebrews had gone to Egypt. Some had remained in the land of Canaan without undergoing the experience of slavery and exodus. Yet, in their willingness to "serve the Lord," the people at Shechem assumed the tradition of the exodus as their own.

A place of union, Shechem was also a place of tribal division. After the death of Solomon in 922 B.C., the area of modern Nablus was the scene of the division of the kingdom of Israel. Ten tribes formed the Northern Kingdom, and the tribe of Benjamin joined the tribe of Judah to make up the Southern Kingdom. Shechem became the capital of the Northern Kingdom, and remained so until the rule of Omri (876-869). In 876 Omri bought a hill about six miles northwest of Shechem:

> **He bought the hill of Samaria from Shemer for two talents of silver; and he fortified the hill, and called the name of the city which he built, Samaria [Shomeron] after the name of Shemer, the owner of the hill.** *(I Kings 16-24)*

For about 150 years after that the name of the new capital, Samaria, came to represent the whole land of the Northern Kingdom, also called Israel, just as Jerusalem came to stand for the entire Southern Kingdom, also called Judah. Then, in 722 B.C., the city and district of Samaria were conquered by the Assyrians. Around thirty thousand Samaritans were forcibly removed from their land and deported to faraway parts of the Assyrian empire, and people from Babylon and other Assyrian regions were settled in their place:

> **And the king of Assyria brought people from Babylon, Cuthah, Avva, Hamath, and Sepharvaim, and placed them in the cities of Samaria instead of the people of Israel; and they took possession of Samaria, and dwelt in its cities.** *(II Kings 17:24)*

Sargon, the King of Assyria and the conqueror of Samaria, tells us in his own record of how he settled in Samaria people from lands which he incorporated into his empire. These new settlers contributed to the origin of the later Samaritans. From this time on, Jews in Samaria were regarded as impure by the Jews of Jerusalem, for they were religiously suspect. Thus, the proverbial hostility between Jews and Samaritans was evident even before the fall of Jerusalem in 586 B.C. and the Babylonian captivity.

We do not have undisputed evidence regarding the time when the temple on Mount Gerizim was built. Some historians think that the Samaritans erected their temple in the fifth century B.C. Others do not think it was built before the Greek conquest of Palestine in 333. We do know, however, that this temple was destroyed in 128 B.C. by the Jewish high priest and civil ruler John Hyrcanus. This act led to a full and final break in relations between Jews and Samaritans.

The ancient city of Samaria was rebuilt by Herod the Great in the first century B.C. It was also renamed Sebaste, to honor the Emperor Augustus (called Sebastos in Greek). Herod's name for the town has survived to the present day in its Arabic form.

At the time of Jesus the Samaritans numbered as many as 750,000, but in the succeeding centuries they fell victim to persecution and conversion. A revolt in Nablus in A.D. 484 brought harsh punishment upon them from the Byzantine Emperor Zeno, who had them removed from Mount Gerizim. This led to another rebellion in 529, which resulted in their virtual extermination by the emperor Justinian. Then when the Muslim armies occupied Palestine, many of the remaining Samaritans accepted Islam. Only in the eighteenth century did some of those who had remained faithful to their religious tradition succeed in purchasing a piece of land on their holy mountain, Gerizim, and in the nineteenth century they secured the title of the mountain and received permission to celebrate there again. But by the turn of this century they numbered only about 150, and marriage between close relatives within the sect threatened them with biological extinction. After the creation of the state of Israel, then, they permitted marriage with Jews provided the partner converted to their own faith.

Today there are about five hundred Samaritans in modern Israel. They live mainly in Nablus, on the slope of Mount Gerizim and near Tel Aviv. Although they publicly imitate the surrounding culture in such matters as dress, for example, they privately safeguard their traditions, living together in one quarter and passing on to their children their language, history and faith in after-school classes.

The past is very real to the Samaritans. They never fail to emphasize all that Mount Gerizim stands for and means to them. A Samaritan once asked a Christian how he understands the words of Psalm 137: "If I forget you, O Jerusalem, let my right hand wither!" The Christian began to answer with a general observation of the meaning of remembering, particularly of remembering Jerusalem in the life of ancient Israel. But the Samaritan insisted that the word "if" in "If I forget you" implies that "the Jews one day may forget Jerusalem." Meanwhile, he declared with assurance, "we can never forget our Mount Gerizim. It is our life, and life cannot be forgotten." The Samaritans do not forget anything. But their historical memory, while preserving their unique form of Judaism, has led to a life of isolation from the larger Jewish community.

Jacob's Well

One uncontested site in Palestine is Jacob's well, on the outskirts of Nablus at the foot of Mount Gerizim. Unlike some other sites, there are not "two wells," one Latin and one Greek; the one well and church is under the protection of the Greek Orthodox Patriarchate of Jerusalem.

The well is close to the village of Askar, which is identified by some as the New Testament Sychar. Other archeologists do not accept this identification and think that the Sychar mentioned in John 4 is a corruption of the original Sychem, i.e., Shechem. The Old Syriac gospels use the name Shechem in place of Sychar. There is no doubt, however, that this is the place where Christ conversed with the Samaritan woman. As he was passing through Samaria—which was not on his usual route from Judea to Galilee—he came to "Sychar," near the field that Jacob had given to his son Joseph. He sat down beside Jacob's well, and soon afterward a Samaritan woman came to draw water for her household.

Jesus said to her, "Give me a drink." For his disciples had gone away into the city to buy food. The Samaritan woman said to him, "How is it that you, a Jew, ask a drink of me, a woman of Samaria? For Jews have no dealings with Samaritans. Jesus answered her, "If you knew the gift of God, and who it is that is saying to you, 'Give me a drink,' you would have asked him, and he would have given you living water." The woman said to him, "Sir, you have nothing to draw with, and the well is deep; where do you get that living water? Are you greater than our father Jacob, who gave us the well, and drank from it himself, and his sons and his cattle?" Jesus said to her, "Every one who drinks of this water will thirst again, but whoever drinks of the water that I shall give him will never thirst; the water that I shall give him will become in him a spring of water welling up to eternal life." The woman said to him, "Sir, give me this water, that I may not thirst, nor come here to draw."

Jesus said to her, "Go, call your husband, and come here." The woman answered him, "I have no husband." Jesus said to her, "You are right in saying, 'I have no husband'; for you have had five husbands, and he whom you now have is not your husband; this you said truly." The woman said to him, "Sir, I perceive that you are a prophet. Our fathers worshiped on this mountain; and you say that in Jerusalem is the place where men ought to worship." Jesus said to her, "Woman, believe me, the hour is coming when neither on this mountain nor in Jerusalem will you worship the Father. You

> worship what you do not know; we worship what we know, for
> salvation is from the Jews. But the hour is coming, and now is, when
> the true worshipers will worship the Father in spirit and truth." The
> woman said to him, "I know that Messiah is coming (he who is called
> Christ); when he comes, he will show us all things." Jesus said to
> her, "I who speak to you am he."   *(John 4:7-26)*

From his conversation with the Samaritan woman, we learn that the well was deep and that it was given by "our father Jacob" (John 4:12, cf. Genesis 33:18). From Jesus' words we know that the well was at Mount Gerizim. At the well, Christ had a clear view of the holy mount of the Samaritans. Again, his words have a special significance when considered in their geographical context.

This conversation reflected the centuries-old hostility between Samaritans and Jews. "How is it that you, a Jew, ask a drink of me, a woman of Samaria?" The evangelist reminds his readers, "For Jews have no dealings with Samaritans" (John 4:9). St Luke also mentions this hostility. On his last journey, when Jesus "set his face to go to Jerusalem," the Samaritans were unwilling to allow him and his disciples to pass through their territory. As he had been rejected in Nazareth, so he was also rejected in the villages of Samaria while on the road leading to his death in Jerusalem:

> When the days drew near for him to be received up, he set his face
> to go to Jerusalem. And he sent messengers ahead of him, who
> went and entered a village of the Samaritans, to make ready for
> him; but the people would not receive him, because his face was set
> toward Jerusalem. And when his disciples James and John saw it,
> they said, "Lord, do you want us to bid fire come down from heaven
> and consume them?" But he turned and rebuked them. And they
> went on to another village.   *(Luke 9:51-56)*

In biblical times the well was on ground level, but now its mouth lies twenty feet below the surface. Also considerably deeper in ancient times, it now goes down about 150 feet. The first church here was built in the fourth century, incorporating an earlier baptistry in its crypt. Today we see a church, begun in 1914 with Russian funds, reconstructing the outlines of the Byzantine church. Construction on this church was halted with the walls half built in 1917, when Russian money dried up after the revolution. The baptistry and the deep well are now kept by a Greek Orthodox monk.

The modern name Nablus reflects the Roman town Neapolis (New City), founded close by after Shechem was finally destroyed in A.D. 70. Roman colonists settled in Neapolis, including a family that, in the first decade of the second century, gave birth to a child who would later be converted to Christianity and become one of the earliest, most important and best known Christian apologists and martyrs—St Justin the Martyr, "the Philosopher."

The date of Justin's conversion to Christianity is uncertain, but it probably took place about 135. Justin himself tells us about his dialogue with an old man on the seashore during the second Jewish revolt against the Romans under the leadership of Bar Kochba (132-135). After outlining the quest for truth, starting with the Stoic philosophers and coming to the Platonists, the old man told him that "long before the time of those reputed philosophers there lived blessed men who were just, and loved by God, men who spoke through the inspiration of the Holy Spirit and predicted events that would take place in the future." He asked Justin to examine these prophets, who pointed to Christ. Justin's journey and search for "true philosophy" ended when he was baptized "into Christ."

Jerusalem: Dome of the Rock and the Mount of Olives

JERUSALEM AND ITS ENVIRONS

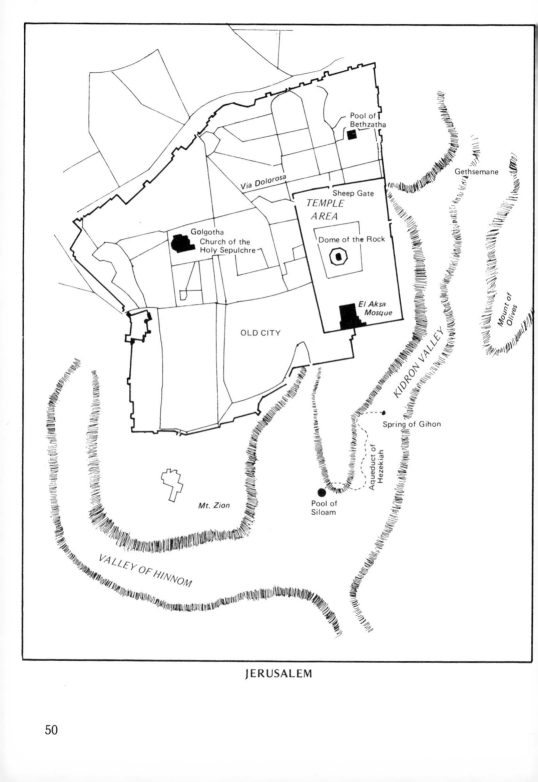

JERUSALEM

Jerusalem

Memorials: Ancient and Modern

From the hills outside Jerusalem, one can see the walls of the old city, with its old and new towers and structures on near and distant hills marking the crossroads of nations, faiths, cultures and historical epochs.

Near the Damascus gate is a fifth or sixth century Armenian mortuary chapel off Hanevi'im, the Street of the Prophets. Beautifully formed birds and plants are displayed on the best-preserved mosaic floor in the country. An inscription in Armenian at the end of the room dedicates the floor to "all Armenians whose names are known to God alone." In the Russian convent on the Mount of Olives, there is another, smaller but beautifully executed mosaic floor, again with an inscription in Armenian.

The nation of Armenia embraced Christianity in the early fourth century, and by the seventh century there were seventy Armenian convents in Jerusalem. Even in 1948 there were eight thousand Armenians living in the old city, and today there are still about two thousand. As one of the oldest continually active groups, they are an important indigenous presence in the holy city. The vespers celebrated in the Cathedral of St James in the Armenian quarter—with the carpeted floor and the many lamps, the disciplined altar boys swinging censers, the deacons and the chanting monks—proved a modern yet timeless reminder of this close-knit, unified tradition.

A modern memorial is Yad Vashem, the Museum of the Holocaust. The visitor enters it along a path called the "Avenue of the Righteous," which is lined with plaques giving the names of Gentiles who had helped or tried to save Jews during World War II. The entrance to the building itself is like a cave, completely black and low ceilinged, with room after room of illuminated exhibits. Displayed are various objects associated with the life of Jewish communities that were destroyed, instruments of destruction, and mementoes of concentration camps, the Warsaw ghetto and the resistance. Most effective are the numerous enlarged photographs, where the eye is captured by a child playing as a soldier approaches or a man as he realizes in desperation that he is doomed. Particular attention is devoted to evidence of resistance, to stress the determination never to go passively to annihilation.

The approach to the museum and the museum itself are worthy and dignified memorials to the millions of innocent victims of the Nazi holocaust. The Holocaust Museum brings to mind all the other victims to whom monuments have not yet been erected. One cannot go through this museum without remembering all the victims and martyrs of different nationalities who were exterminated by the same totalitarian power of Nazi Germany or by those who followed the same policy of genocide. Hundreds of thousands of Orthodox Serbs, for instance, were murdered in the most horrifying manner in the so-called Independent Croatian State during World War II, some burned alive in their churches. This was a holocaust in its literal meaning.

The Nazis were bearers of a spirit of a new and aggressive paganism. Their religion lacked any element of transcendence; they themselves played the role of God. The Holocaust Museum is a place to remember that the doctrine of purity of race and blood led to unprecedented bloodshed and extermination. The concept of race and fanatic nationalism released demonic powers. To remember is to hope that the history of the tragic 1930s and 40s will be overcome by a new history, one in which humans will not arrogate to themselves divine authority over life and death.

The Temple Mount and Mount Zion

In the Bible, the city of Jerusalem is often referred to by the name of the hill on which the ancient city was built—Mount Zion. Today, we see the city situated chiefly on two hills, one on the east and another on the west. The hill on the west side is more impressive than the one on the east. For this reason, in the time of Constantine the hill on the west was identified as Zion, the hill on which the ancient Jebusite city was located. Now, however, it is accepted that the hill on the east was the site of the tenth-century B.C. city of David and Solomon, and of the holiest shrine of ancient Judaism, the Temple.

The Temple site was first established around 1000 B.C., when King David moved his capital from Hebron to Jerusalem, the Jebusite city situated on the southern end of the eastern hill. He also bought the threshing floor of Araunah the Jebusite, as the Lord had commanded him through the prophet Gad.

> **And when Araunah looked down, he saw the king and his servants coming on toward him; and Araunah went forth, and did obeisance to the king with his face to the ground. And Araunah said, "Why has my lord the king come to his servant?" David said, "To buy the threshing floor of you, in order to build an altar to the Lord". . . David bought the threshing floor and the oxen for fifty shekels of silver.** *(II Samuel 24:20-24)*

On this spot Solomon built the Temple.

The Babylonians destroyed the Temple in 587 B.C. When the Jews returned from their Babylonian exile in 538, however, they immediately began the reconstruction of the Temple, along the lines of the Temple of Solomon. But it required more physical effort and material sacrifice than they could give to recover the splendor and beauty of the first Temple. Some old men "who had seen the first house, wept with a loud voice when they saw the foundation of this house being laid" (Ezra 3:12).

The grandeur of the Temple was recaptured only under Herod the Great. Resented by the Jews, he tried to earn their loyalty and cooperation by starting a complete renovation of the Temple in 20 B.C. He was very methodical in his preparations for this enormous and sensitive task. For instance, he did not begin until as many as a thousand priests had been trained in the building trade, for only priests could be allowed to work on the inner section, the Court of the Priests. Outside this court was to be the Court of the Israelites, where all Jewish men could enter, and still further from the sanctuary was to be the Women's Court. Stones with inscriptions in Greek warning that any Gentile who enters the Court of Israel, the sacred precinct, will be punished by death still survive from Herod's Temple. One is in the Ottoman Museum in Istanbul; fragments of the second are in the Rockefeller Museum in Jerusalem.

Herod built walls with enormous stone blocks to mark and protect the area of the Temple Mount. About ten percent of the western retaining wall still survives. This is the Western Wall, or Wailing Wall, the most sacred site of

Western wall of Solomon's Temple,
the "Wailing Wall" in Jerusalem today.

Judaism today. On the southeast corner of the retaining walls was the "pinnacle," which recalls the second temptation of Jesus: "Then the devil took him to the holy city, and set him on the pinnacle of the Temple" (Matthew 4:5).

According to rabbinical tradition, "He who has not seen the Temple of Herod has never in his life seen a beautiful building." Of the city itself it was said: "Anyone who has not seen Jerusalem in all its beauty has never beheld a great and lovely city in all his life." Jesus also referred to the grandeur of the Temple, during the last week of his public ministry. One of his disciples said to him, as Jesus was coming out of the Temple, "Look, Teacher, what wonderful stones and what wonderful buildings!" But Jesus answered: "Do you see these great buildings? There will not be left here one stone upon another, that will not be thrown down" (Mark 13:1-2). And in A.D. 70, just a few years after the Temple was completed, the Romans finally destroyed it.

Hadrian, a Roman emperor of the second century, erected a temple to the Roman god Jupiter over the ruins of Herod's Temple. This irreverent act, together with his attempt to build a Greco-Roman city called Aelia Capitolina on the site of Jerusalem and his edict forbidding circumcision, led to the second Jewish revolt in 132. The revolt was totally crushed three years later, and Jerusalem again suffered the wrath of the Romans. From the time of Hadrian through Byzantine rule, the Arab conquest and the Turkish occupation, right on up to the Six-day War of 1967, Jews were excluded from the place where the first and second temples had stood.

When Palestine and Jerusalem were part of the Byzantine empire, from the fourth to the seventh century, Christians erected many churches and monasteries in Jerusalem and throughout the area. Yet they never attempted to construct anything on the site of the Temple. The Temple Mount, which was traditionally designated as the Mount Moriah of Abraham's sacrifice (Genesis 22), was totally neglected and abandoned in this period. For the Byzantine Christians, the ruins of the Temple witnessed to the truth of Jesus' prediction of its destruction and to the futility of the old Israel, whose Temple did not enclose the true Holy of Holies.

Many important events of gospel history occurred on the Temple Mount. In particular, it was here that Jesus was presented in the Temple:

> **And when time came for their purification according to the law of Moses, they brought him up to Jerusalem to present him to the Lord (as it is written in the law of the Lord, "Every male that opens the womb shall be called holy to the Lord") and to offer a sacrifice according to what is said in the law of the Lord, "a pair of turtle-**

doves, or two young pigeons." Now there was a man in Jerusalem, whose name was Simeon, and this man was righteous and devout, looking for the consolation of Israel, and the Holy Spirit was upon him. And it had been revealed to him by the Holy Spirit that he should not see death before he had seen the Lord's Christ. And inspired by the Spirit he came into the temple; and when the parents brought in the child Jesus, to do for him according to the custom of the law, he took him up in his arms and blessed God and said,

"Lord, now lettest thou thy servant depart in peace, according to thy word;
for mine eyes have seen thy salvation
which thou has prepared in the presence of all peoples,
a light for revelation to the Gentiles,
and for glory to thy people Israel." *(Luke 2:22-32)*

The Christians of Jerusalem, where the feast of the Presentation was inaugurated in the late fourth century, did not celebrate the feast at the Temple site, but at the Church of the Resurrection.

Two checkpoints must be passed before entering Haram esh-Sharif, the mount itself. This is where the temples of Solomon and Herod had been erected, and today it is the third holiest place of Islam. The Temple Mount covers thirty-five acres of elevated ground within the old city wall. There are two great mosques on the mount, the El-Aksa and the Dome of the Rock.

The El-Aksa Mosque is a basilica built in the eighth century. Its large, almost square hall with seven lines of pillars is completely covered with magnificent oriental carpets. It was here that Sadat came to pray on his peace mission to Israel in 1977.

The pride of the Temple Mount is the Dome of the Rock. This shrine was built under Abd el-Malik in 688-691 by Byzantine Syrian Christians, who were hired to apply their skills to this new purpose of creating one of the masterpieces of Islamic art. Constructed according to mathematical relationships of circles and squares, it is one of the most successful examples of the Byzantine-style rotunda, with light filtering through the colored glass in the dome highlighting the stones in the mosaic decorations.

The Dome of the Rock challenged Judaism by occupying the site of the Temple and the great rock traditionally associated with Abraham and Isaac. The rock may also have served as the place of sacrifice in the Temple.

The Dome was even more of a challenge to Christianity. Simple Muslim shepherds had been awe-struck by the Byzantine Christian monuments;

therefore, the Muslins wanted to send a counter-message. The octagonal design and even the workmen were borrowed from Byzantine Christendom, but the message of the mosaics inside was clear. The diadems, breastplates and flowers come from Byzantine icons and court dress—the spoils of the victor. The main inscription around the dome says, in part, "Believe in God and his apostles and say not Three . . . God is only one God." Because of the way the stones are tilted, the subject seems to emerge from the background in high relief.

Nearby is the Islamic Museum, which contains many Byzantine columns and sculptures that had been reused on the Temple Mount, as well as tiles, screens and other objects from the mosques. Among the highlights is a Quran that was supposedly copied by Muhammad's great grandson onto parchment.

Mount Zion: The Coenaculum

Across the Old City from the Temple Mount lies Mount Zion. Located just outside the Zion Gate, Mount Zion was the site of the largest fifth century Byzantine church, the "Mother of all Churches," which has been totally destroyed.

A huge, black-domed, round Catholic Church of the Dormition dominates this southeast hill outside the modern walls. Below it, the traveler goes through a courtyard to a passageway, then turns left into the room of the tomb of David. Men are offered yarmulkes at the entrance of the tomb, which is venerated as a Jewish religious shrine. But there is no doubt that David was not buried here. As already noted, in the fourth century the area known as Zion shifted from the eastern part of the city to the west. There is an international yeshiva next to the shrine.

To reach the Coenaculum, the room traditionally regarded as the site of the Last Supper, one must climb a stairway in a Muslim building and enter a vaulted room just above the tomb. According to a fourth century Jerusalem Christian tradition, this was also the place where Christ appeared to his disciples after his resurrection for the first time (John 20:19). It is also associated with Pentecost (Acts 2:1). Nothing in the room survives from the first century. The building itself is typical of twelfth-century Crusader architecture, and the gothic vaults were built in the fourteenth century by Latin architects imported from Cyprus. No attempt is made to set the scene as it would have appeared at the Last Supper, and no sign, inside or outside, identifies the room, yet pilgrims and tourists still find it. The original room was part of a private house in the time of Jesus, and probably was located somewhere within the present building.

The "upper room" belongs neither to Latin nor Greek Christians but to Muslims. There is a story that when St Sava of Serbia visited the Holy Land on his first pilgrimage in 1228 or 1229, he was saddened to learn that one of the most sacred places of the Christian Church was in Muslim hands. Therefore he bought the place with gold and made it a possession of the Serbian Church. Soon afterward the Upper Room apparently reverted to the Muslims once again. Pope Clement VI (1342-52) negotiated with the Muslims to allow the Franciscans to restore the Upper Room, but in the sixteenth century it was converted into a mosque. Now neither Christians nor Muslims may hold services here.

Although there is no way to substantiate exactly where the Last Supper and Pentecost took place, we do have a very strong unbroken Christian tradition attesting to its genuineness. No other place mentioned competes with Mount Zion. Even after the destruction of Jerusalem, in 70 and 134, memory of this site persisted.

The Pools of Bethzatha and Siloam

Near the Temple Mount, at St Stephen's Gate, stands a lovely Crusader church of the twelfth century named for St Anne. Not far from it is the place where Jesus healed a man who had been ill for thirty-eight years:

> **After this there was a feast of the Jews, and Jesus went up to Jerusalem. Now there is in Jerusalem by the sheep gate a pool, in Hebrew called Bethzatha, which has five porticoes. In these lay a multitude of invalids, blind, lame, paralyzed. One man was there, who had been ill for thirty-eight years. When Jesus saw him and knew that he had been lying there a long time, he said to him, "Do you want to be healed?" The sick man answered him, "Sir, I have no man to put me into the pool when the water is troubled, and while I am going another steps down before me." Jesus said to him, "Rise, take up your pallet, and walk." And at once the man was healed, and he took up his pallet and walked.** *(John 5:1-9)*

The pool originally supplied the Temple with water. In the period of Roman Hellenism, this was known as a place of healing as well as cleansing.

Archeological excavations done at the site of this Sheep Pool, and interpretations based upon them, throw much light upon this gospel text. Two pools and six caves have been identified, as well as eleven small stone pools. There are additional caves under St Anne's Church.

What is the pool with five porticos, referred to in the Gospel? According to Frs Bénoit and Duprer, specialists in the archeology of Jerusalem, they are not the two great pools, which were of irregular shape and considerable depth, therefore not suitable for immersing a paralytic. Jerzy Klinger, in a recent article, summarizes the prevailing view that five therapeutic centers were located in the caves, "where hydrotherapy was practiced in the small stone containers that still remain, and which were filled from the large cistern." This therapeutic center was active during the public ministry of Christ and was dedicated to Asclepius, the pagan god of healing. In other words, the Pool of Bethzatha was a pagan healing sanctuary.

Could there have been a pagan center of healing in Jerusalem? In this period Hellenistic influences were strong throughout the area, particularly affecting the upper levels of society. Moreover, the pagan center of healing was not located within the walls of ancient Jerusalem but outside them.

A second question which Klinger discusses arises in regard to Christ's relation to this pagan sanctuary. Jesus entered a pagan center, not a Jewish one, and here he performed the miracle of healing. Here once again we see the contact of Jesus with the Gentile world, and an indication that not only was he the fulfillment of the Old Testament but of pagan expectations as well. The gospel text should be reread in the light of this archeological evidence, as well as of the literary and historical sources available to us.

With the conversion of Constantine the Great, Byzantine Christians in the fourth century built a church which incorporated the two pools and dedicated it to the Theotokos, who was traditionally believed to have lived in the vicinity, as well as to the miracle of the healing of the paralytic. Near the ruins of this church, which was destroyed in the eleventh century, the Crusaders built the Church of St Anne. A chapel was built on the ruins, with a staircase leading down to the site of the miracle at the pool. It takes quite a lot of imagination to appreciate the meaning of these ruins in the tangle of history, building and destruction, and appropriation by different faiths and denominations. In the garden of the church is a bust of Cardinal Levigerie, the founder of the White Fathers, who had conducted a school here for Arab Melchite seminarians until the middle of this century.

Another pool that is important in the Gospel narrative is the Pool of Siloam, located down the slope from the Dung Gate in the oldest part of Jerusalem, known as "David's City." The pool is fifty-eight feet long and eighteen feet wide. Here Jesus healed the blind man:

Pool of Siloam

As he passed by, he saw a man blind from his birth. And his disciples asked him, "Rabbi, who sinned, this man or his parents, that he was born blind?" Jesus answered, "It was not that this man sinned, or his parents, but that the works of God might be made manifest in him. We must work the works of him who sent me, while it is day; night comes, when no one can work. As long as I am in the world, I am the light of the world." As he said this, he spat on the ground and made clay of the spittle and anointed the man's eyes with the clay, saying to him, "Go, wash in the pool of Siloam" (which means Sent). So he sent and washed and came back seeing. The neighbors and those who had seen him before as a beggar, said, "Is not this the man who used to sit and beg?" Some said, "It is he"; others say, "No, but he is like him." He said, "I am the man." They said to him, "Then how were your eyes opened?" He answered, "The man called Jesus made clay and anointed my eyes and said to me, 'Go to Siloam and wash'; so I went and washed and received my sight." They said to him, "Where is he?" He said, "I do not know."

(John 9:1-12)

At one end of the pool, one can see the entrance to an ancient tunnel, the aqueduct of Hezekiah, through which water from the spring of Gihon was brought to the pool. Extensive archeological explorations have been carried out here. Along the road to Gihon there is a sign pointing to excavations made by the archeologist Kathleen Kenyon, who had also worked outside Jericho. Here she has uncovered a Jebusite wall of the eighteenth century B.C., which indicates how the borders of the city have shifted over the years. The spring of Gihon, now far outside the walls of the Old City, was the first center for the most ancient foundations of the city.

59

The Church of the Resurrection and Golgotha

Visits to the Temple Mount and Mount Zion are good preparation for seeing the Church of the Resurrection. Also known as the Church of the Holy Sepulchre, it is the most sacred and the most perplexing of all the Christian holy sites in Jerusalem.

The church is located in a crowded area, with only a small courtyard separating it from the other surrounding buildings. The road to it passes through the souq or bazaar, near the Jaffa Gate, where shopkeepers and peddlers cram every inch of the sides of the walkway, hawking their souvenirs, clothes and other wares.

To reach Golgotha, the place of the crucifixion, one must ascend a spiral staircase to the right of the entrance. The main altar here is in the care of the Greek Orthodox Patriarchate, and next to it is a Franciscan chapel.

In the Chapel of Adam, below Golgotha, the visitor can see through a glass plate a crack in the bedrock. The name of the chapel has its origin in the story which serves as a symbol that Adam was buried on the spot over which the cross of Christ stood. In the icon of the crucifixion in the Orthodox Church, the victory over death is symbolized by a cave at the foot of the cross, where Adam's skull appears out of a split rock. According to the gospels, when Jesus yielded up his spirit, "the rocks were split" and "the tombs also were opened" (Matthew 27:51-52). The legend and the icon express a profound religious truth, illustrating the relationship between Adam and Christ, between the first and the last Adam. "For as in Adam all die, so also in Christ shall all be made alive" (I Corinthians 15:22). The first Adam is redeemed by the last Adam. The icon of the resurrection depicts the risen Christ pulling Adam and Eve out of Hades.

The center of worship in the church is the Holy Sepulchre, the place of the resurrection. The tomb is guarded by Greek Orthodox monks. Around in back of the shrine is a stone, which remains from the tomb erected by Constantine, a survival from the general destruction of the church in the eleventh century and now under Coptic protection.

"Golgotha" is an Aramaic word which translates as "the place of the skull." The word Calvary comes from the Latin term for Golgotha, Calvariae locus. The site of the crucifixion was an elevation, a rocky hill shaped like a skull, which was located outside the walls of Jerusalem at the time of Christ. At first the modern traveler is disconcerted therefore to find Golgotha inside the walls of the old city. But the city we see now differs markedly from the walled city of Christ's time. In the first century, Jerusalem was protected on the northern side by two walls, and Golgotha was outside the second wall, yet probably close enough to the inner wall so that people could watch the crucifixion from it. The walls of the old city that stand today were built in the sixteenth century by the Turks, erected to protect the old city, which by that time included the Church of the Resurrection.

The Holy Land Hotel, located outside the old city, has on its property a model of first-century Jerusalem, carefully prepared according to the most recent research and scholarship. In this model one can see the outline of the old walls, which were much more extensive than the present walls of the old city. Golgotha, "just outside the wall"—the second wall—is found in the model at the place of the Holy Sepulchre, which is now nearer the middle of the old city. Other important landmarks were Herod's palace, which took up almost an entire side of the city opposite the Temple Mount, and the magnificent Temple itself. Down from the Temple lay the Pool of Siloam. This model of the impressive new Hellenistic city serves as an excellent correction to the elegant decay and the fragmentary traces we now see in modern Jerusalem.

The tomb in which Joseph of Arimathea laid the body of Christ was very near the place of the crucifixion (John 19:41). Many women attentively watched the burial, planning to come to the tomb and anoint Christ's body after the Sabbath. It was also a Jewish custom to pray at the tombs of holy men, and the followers of Jesus in Jerusalem used to pray and perform liturgical celebrations at the location of his tomb. Thus, from the very beginning of the Christian era the disciples of Christ venerated their master's tomb, at the site where some of them had actually witnessed the burial.

Soon after the crucifixion, through the efforts of Herod Agrippa I, Jerusalem was enlarged, and it is possible that already by A.D. 44 Golgotha was within the walls of the expanded city. After the Emperor Hadrian razed Jerusalem and its old walls following the second Jewish revolt, his new city, Aelia Capitolina, definitely included the site of Golgotha. When Melito, the bishop of Sardis in Lydia, made a pilgrimage to Palestine around 170, he wrote that Jesus was crucified in the city of Jerusalem—that is, within the walls of Hadrian's Aelia Capitolina.

After the destruction of the old Jerusalem, Hadrian covered both Golgotha and the tomb of Christ with statues of pagan deities. According to Eusebius, the whole area of Golgotha was destroyed before the idols were erected. The Romans brought a large amount of earth from distant places to cover the Holy of Holies of the Christian religion and tried to erase the place of the skull by leveling it and raising the ground around it. After paving it all with stone, they built what Eusebius called "a gloomy shrine of lifeless idols." St

Jerome, who settled in Bethlehem in 386 and lived there until his death in 420, writes in his *Letter 58* that the site of the resurrection was occupied by the figure of Jupiter, while on the rock where the cross stood was a marble statue of Venus. He adds that other places linked with the life and ministry of Christ were also transformed by the pagans into shrines to their gods. "Even my own Bethlehem" was "overshadowed by a grove of Tammuz, that is of Adonis," he lamented. But the Christians of Jerusalem preserved the memory of the location of Golgotha from the reign of Hadrian, who died in 138, until that of Constantine, who became the first Christian Roman emperor in 313.

When Constantine decided to build the Church of the Resurrection, he gave orders that the rubble brought by the Romans to Golgotha be removed and the idols destroyed. The churches commemorating the crucifixion and the resurrection were then located where the tradition of the local Christians remembered that the events took place. Eusebius reported that the construction would have been easier on a nearby site, but the local believers insisted on the exact locations as sacred memory had preserved them. Jesus' crucifixion had been a public act of the Roman authorities. Thus, we can certainly assume that there were first-century Christians in Jerusalem who had seen the execution. They remembered the very places where Jesus died and was buried, and passed on their memory to succeeding generations.

John Wilkinson, in *Jerusalem as Jesus Knew It,* writes that Eusebius' account of the placement of the churches "rings true" for three main reasons. First, it shows how much Christians were concerned with the holy places before Constantine became the first Christian emperor and had the churches built on the sites linked with Jesus' life and work. Second, the site that was excavated under Constantine's orders was inside the city walls at that time. If the tradition of the location of Golgotha had not been quite firm, stresses Wilkinson, then there would have been a strong temptation to look for Golgotha outside the walls as they then stood. Finally, the site that was chosen has since been proved by excavations to be a first-century tomb area. This site, he concludes, "is the only one which can with any probability be regarded as the place in which Jesus was buried." And this is the site on which the Church of the Resurrection was built.

The Church of the Resurrection was completed and dedicated in 335. We have references to this event in the hymns sung on the eve of the feast of the Exaltation of the Life-giving Cross in the Orthodox Church. One of the hymns runs as follows: "The Tree of true life was planted in the place of the skull, and upon it hast Thou, the eternal King, worked salvation in the midst of the earth.

Exalted today, it sanctifies the ends of the world, and the Church of the Resurrection celebrates its dedication."

When Egeria made her pilgrimage to Jerusalem in the fourth century, she saw the structure erected by Constantine. It consisted of a covered apsidal basilica, the Martyrium (Place of Witness), an open courtyard, and opposite the basilica a rotunda, which she called the Anastasis (Resurrection), enclosing the tomb. Egeria gives us a vivid picture of a baptism performed here on the eve of Easter: "The newly baptized come into the Anastasis, and any of the faithful who wish to hear the mysteries . . . No catechumen comes in." Then, during the time from Easter to the eighth day of the feast, "after the dismissal has taken place in the church, and they have come with singing into the Anastasis—the bishop stands leaning against the inner screen in the cave of the Anastasis, and interprets all that takes place in Baptism . . . as he does so, the applause is so loud that it can be heard outside the church. Indeed the way he expounds the mysteries and interprets them cannot fail to move his hearers."

Instruction on all the scriptures was given from six to nine in the morning throughout Lent. Also during this period of preparation and fasting, the bishop would devote three hours each day to teaching the basic facts of the faith. "At ordinary services, when the bishop sits and preaches," Egeria continues, describing what she had seen to her sisters in the convent, "the faithful utter exclamations, but when they come and hear him explaining the catechesis, their exclamations are far louder, God is my witness; and when it is related and interpreted like this they ask questions on each point." All this probably occurred in the church she called the Martyrium, on the site of Golgotha. Undoubtedly this church community was very alive, and very much a scriptural church. Unfortunately, the tradition she records has long been broken.

Constantine's church withstood damage by fire from the Persians in 614 and the Muslim conquest of 638, only to be finally destroyed by the mad Caliph al-Hakim in 1009. This is the same al-Hakim who, as we mentioned earlier, is revered by the Druse. Considered to have been mentally sick, "one of the most eccentric men ever to have wielded power in Islam," he ordered his governor to demolish the Church of the Resurrection and to remove "all trappings of Christian splendor." The wanton and thorough destruction of the church, which included the smashing of the tomb of Christ into debris, was one of the immediate causes of the Crusades. Although forty years later the Byzantine Emperor Monomachus allotted funds for the restoration of the church, it was greatly reduced in size, and only the Anastasis (Resurrection)

Church of the Resurrection

rotunda was somewhat fully restored. When the Crusaders came to Jerusalem in 1099, they introduced many changes in their own restoration of the church, including a roof over the open court, and they began calling it the Church of the Holy Sepulchre. What we see today is essentially the twelfth-century Romanesque church that the Crusaders completed in 1149.

Since the beginning of the nineteenth century, the church has suffered considerably from fire, earthquake and neglect. But in 1959, the Christian groups with traditional rights here, including Greeks, Latins and Armenians, began working together on the restoration of the church. The aim of the present restorers is to rebuild the church on the pattern of the Crusader structure of the twelfth century.

When church dignitaries celebrate in the Church of the Resurrection, they are preceded by a *kavass*, a fezzed attendant, pounding the floor with his staff and clearing the way for the religious procession. Since the time of Saladin, tradition has it, Muslims have been the custodians of the Church of the Resurrection. The keys to the church are traditionally kept by one family, passing on the duties from father to son. Over the years, the Muslims have had to keep peace among the warring Christian groups in the church and to regulate their relations. Greeks, Latins, Armenians, Syrians, Ethiopians and Copts all have places of worship here and rights, defined in an 1852 document still in effect. Everything in the church, starting with lamps and icons, has its recognized owner. What part of the church belongs to whom is precisely stated, and the responsibilities of each particular group are clearly explained.

Although insistence on their rights on the part of each community reflects long-standing divisions between the churches, there is now more harmony in the Church of the Resurrection than the occasional visitor or ordinary pilgrim might perceive. The diverse groups have become more accepting of the rights of others. And diversity itself need not lead to hostility—after all, the early church was also diverse in its organization and ecclesiastical traditions. The present cooperation among Greeks, Latins and Armenians is a tentative witness to what may be an end to the tension and hostility among the Christian groups in Jerusalem.

Very close by the Church of the Resurrection is the headquarters of the Russian Orthodox Church outside of Russia (the Synod), which has custody of some of the prerevolutionary Russian holdings in Palestine. At the "excavations," as the administrative center is called, the main exhibit is the threshold of the Judgment Gate, through which Christ walked to his crucifixion. This site was excavated by Archimandrite Antonin Kapustin in 1883. Although the stone's authenticity is disputed by some modern archeologists, others regard it as one of the rare authentic remains. The gate was part of Hadrian's temple wall, which formed the western facade of the atrium of Constantine's basilica. There were three doorways cut into the wall, and the door we saw here was the south door. This is an unseen or hidden part of the Church of the Resurrection. It is typical of the jigsaw puzzle one has to put together to visualize the meaningful past of these monuments.

Within the complex of the Church of the Resurrection, monophysite Ethiopian monks have established a monastery on the roof of St. Helena's Chapel. This monastery is but a cluster of mud huts in the ruins of a medieval cloister. The tall and angular Ethiopian monks, dressed in white, are poor but dignified. They are seen throughout the city, at shrines and churches where they come to pray. These monks add an authentic note of Christian poverty and reverence that seems lacking in many Christian institutions in the holy city.

The Monastery of the Holy Cross

On the heights of new Jerusalem, to the west of the city, stand the campus of Hebrew University, the Knesset and the Israel Museum, with the Shrine of the Book—built for the Dead Sea Scrolls—in the courtyard of the museum. The stark, white cupola-shaped shrine, intended to represent the containers in which the scrolls were kept, was designed by Frederick Kiessler.

During our visit, the Israel Museum was displaying a brand new exhibit: a very large Byzantine mosaic floor, discovered in Gaza. It had been removed from there in pieces and reassembled in the downstairs part of the museum. The finely preserved decorations, the Greek inscriptions and particularly an interesting mounted figure in the center made it a treasure indeed. Many relics of the Byzantine past, such as this Gaza mosaic and the monastic complex at Kursi, are only now coming to light under the chisels of archeologists.

The main collections of Judaica in the Museum are reproductions of synagogues from different parts of the world, robes and other articles of clothing, and Torahs. At times one can see a living exhibit: archeologists seated at tables at different stages in the process of reassembling shattered pots. The bookstore contains a good assortment of books on archeology and art in Hebrew, English and European languages.

Looking toward the old city from the Israel Museum, one can see the Monastery of the Holy Cross, a walled, fortress-like complex in what is now the new part of Jerusalem. There is an elaborate legend concerning a tree that grew on this site and provided the wood for the cross of Christ. According to tradition the first church here was built by King Tatian of Georgia (466-499), whose nation had been baptized in the fourth century. A sixth-century structure built under Justinian can still be discerned, but the building we now see is a monastery founded by King Bagrat of Georgia between 1039 and 1056. The Georgians were on good terms with the Mamluk rulers of Palestine and also with the Tartars, but in 1685, after the Russian conquest of Georgia, they were obliged to sell the monastery to the Patriarch of Jerusalem. It is still one of the most splendid monuments in this area and a masterpiece of Georgian art, especially of fresco painting.

The frescoes have been greatly restored, as part of a process that is still going on under the auspices of the Israel Museum. The dark blue of the backgrounds is the dominant color, but other colors are also clear and striking. The figures are individually presented and full of character. Particularly noteworthy is a fresco portraying the visitation of Mary to Elizabeth— beneath the flowing, merging garments, Elizabeth in particular is perceptibly pregnant. In another section, Peter and Paul are shown together, their iconic characteristics very recognizable and both human and original. The great Georgian poet Shoto Rustaveli is buried here, and both he and Queen Tamar are portrayed on one pillar as donors. Above the pillars is a particularly gripping depiction of the annunciation to Joseph, who is crouching down and shielding himself with his arm from the archangel. On the pillars are images of "pillars of the Church," such as the great monastic leaders Euthymius and Saba, and St Cyril of Alexandria, with a black beard and cap. Over the west door is a striking image of a monk. Blindfolded and chained, he stands in front of the cross and holds a torch. The monk is blind to the world and chained by his pledge of obedience, but with the promise of the cross behind him he carries a torch in his hand, the light to the world.

St Cyril of Jerusalem, who was bishop of the city from c.349 to 386, makes constant references in his catechetical instructions to "the holy wood of the cross." We also have an account of the veneration of the true cross in the fourth century from Egeria's visit to Jerusalem, when the cross was offered for veneration on Good Friday. A gold and silver box containing the wood of the cross was brought to the bishop, opened, and a piece of the wood taken out and placed on a table. Then, Egeria continues: "The bishop sits with his hands resting on either end of it and holds it down, and the deacons round him keep watch over it. They guard it like this because what happens now is that all the people, catechumens as well as faithful, come up one by one to the table. They stoop down over it, kiss the Wood, and move on. But on one occasion (I don't know when) one of them bit off a piece of the holy Wood and stole it away, and for this reason the deacons stand around and keep watch in case anyone dares to do the same again."

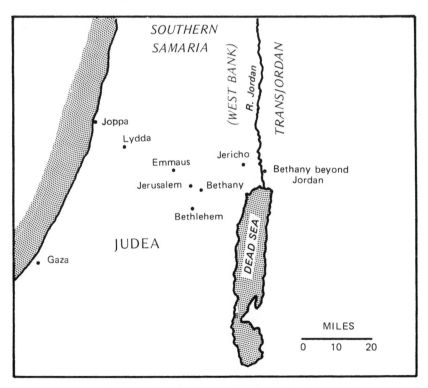

JERUSALEM AND SURROUNDINGS

Bethlehem - Church of the Nativity

After the Church of the Resurrection, the second most important church that Constantine built was the Church of the Nativity, located over the cave of the nativity in Bethlehem.

Bethlehem was the place, according to promise, where the Messiah was to be born (Micah 5:2), but at the time of his birth it was an insignificant village. The apocryphal *Protoevangelium of James* speaks of a cave in which Jesus was born. It was a common practice then to build a house right in front of a cave. The tradition of the nativity taking place in the cave was affirmed in the second century by St Justin. In the third century, Origen and Eusebius also cited this local tradition, and indicated that this particular location had been venerated from the beginning of Christianity. This continuous memory makes the cave at Bethlehem one of the best attested early Christian sites, recognized before Queen Helena's arrival in the fourth century. The main church protects the oldest continuously venerated object in Christendom. It is a relatively well-preserved relic of the grandeur of the past, suffering considerably today from the listlessness of the Christian groups exercising their rights there.

Bethlehem today is an Arab town in the occupied zone. The women still wear their distinctive dresses, although very few are veiled, and they carry baskets on their heads. Manger Square is a parking lot surrounded by a mixture of buildings: monasteries, mosques, and souvenir stores.

The entry to the church shows its history. Justinian (527-565) enlarged Constantine's church and replaced most of it in the process, although the original mosaic floor was excavated in 1934. Justinian's church had three entrances, of which only the central one, now walled up, is still visible. In the twelfth century the Crusaders reduced the size of the archway when they restored the facade. The entry was again reduced in the Ottoman period to the present low square to prevent looters from driving carts into the church. We had to bend down considerably to enter the building.

The structure of the church, with its four rows of red limestone pillars, remains as it was in the time of Justinian. It is an impressive, large basilica in the Byzantine style. Figures of saints painted by the Crusaders are still dimly visible on some of the pillars. Above the pillars on the south side are remnants of twelfth-century mosaics devoted to the ecumenical councils. Below them, on both sides of the nave, are picturesque mosaic illustrations of the genealogies of Jesus according to Matthew and Luke.

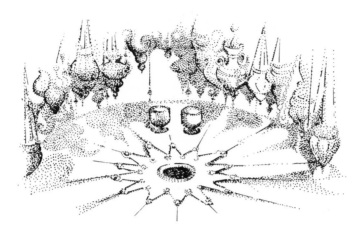

Bethlehem: Grotto in the Church of the Nativity, marking the birthplace of Christ.

The main altar belongs to the Greek Orthodox Church, and one side chapel is held by the Armenians, who also have access to the Grotto of the Nativity. Here the place of the nativity is marked by a star-shaped metal piece set in the floor beneath the altar. A separate Roman Catholic chapel lies to the side. Services are scheduled by agreement between the participating Christian communities, and must be celebrated to preserve their right there. While services are in progress, no one is allowed to approach and venerate the star.

Another section of caves lies to the east of the Grotto. These are particularly associated with St Jerome, who lived here for many years before his death in 420. In these caves, he translated the Bible into Latin (his translation served as the basis for the Vulgate Bible) and wrote many other studies.

The Mount of Olives

The Kidron Valley separates Jerusalem from the Mount of Olives. This valley has been traditionally identified as the Valley of Jehoshaphat, where, according to the third chapter of the book of the prophet Joel, God will gather all the nations and will enter into judgment with them. The Kidron is on the east side of the city, and to the west of Jerusalem is the valley of Hinnom. These two valleys meet in the southeast. We have references to both in the gospels. The Kidron is mentioned in John 18:1: "When Jesus had spoken these words (the Last Discourse), he went forth with his disciples across the Kidron valley, where there was a garden." The Hinnom is related to Gehenna in the synoptic gospels. This valley is the place where in ancient times the refuse from the city was burned. Its Hebrew name, Ge-Hinnom, became corrupted to Gehenna—which serves as an image of hell, the place of eternal punishment, in the synoptic gospels. In the Sermon on the Mount, Christ says that whoever says to his brother "You fool!" will be "liable to the hell (*Gehenna*) of fire" (Matthew 5:22). The same image appears in Mark 9:43: "And if your hand causes you to sin, cut it off; it is better for you to enter life maimed than with two hands to go to hell (*Gehenna*)."

Garden of Gethsemane

The garden of Gethsemane, located on the western slope of the Mount of Olives across the Kidron valley, has a Latin and an Orthodox church. The Latin Church of All Nations preserves the black marble outline of a fourth century church, which Egeria described as "elegant," and which commemorates the place of Christ's distress and arrest:

> And they went to a place which was called Gethsemane; and he said to his disciples, "Sit here, while I pray." And he took with him Peter and James and John, and began to be greatly distressed and troubled. And he said to them, "My soul is very sorrowful, even to death; remain here, and watch." And going a little farther, he fell on the ground and prayed that, if it were possible, the hour might pass from him. And he said, "Abba, Father, all things are possible to thee; remove this cup from me; yet not what I will, but what thou wilt." And he came and found them sleeping, and he said to Peter, "Simon, are you asleep? Could you not watch one hour? Watch and pray that you may not enter into temptation; the spirit indeed is willing, but the flesh is weak." And again he went away and prayed,

saying the same words. And again he came and found them sleeping, for their eyes were very heavy; and they did not know what to answer him. And he came the third time, and said to them, "Are you still sleeping and taking your rest? It is enough; the hour has come; the Son of man is betrayed into the hands of sinners. Rise, let us be going; see, my betrayer is at hand." *(Mark 14:32-42)*

In front of the altar of this Church is a large rock, on which, according to tradition, Christ prayed.

Gethsemane is full of ancient places of veneration. One cave is identified as the place where the disciples rested while waiting for Jesus, who was praying on the night of his arrest. A church commemorates the place where Jesus wept. Almost every stone, cave, flight of steps or tomb has been venerated for over fifteen centuries. One long-time resident, observing how different churches and institutions argue about who possesses the stones Jesus actually stood or sat on, exclaimed, "My goodness! Couldn't he have stood or sat on more than one of these stones?" It is difficult to know for certain whether the modern grove that bears the name of Gethsemane is actually the site of Jesus' agony. But if it is not the site of his prayer and arrest, it all must have taken place somewhere in the immediate area.

The olive trees in the garden are particularly evocative, although it is unlikely that any are over a thousand years old. Looking up from the trees, one has a clear view of the Golden Gate, through which the Messiah was traditionally supposed to have entered Jerusalem on Palm Sunday, although there are other gates with this claim. There are many legends connected with the

*Olive trees in the
Garden of Gethsemane*

Golden Gate, which opens directly onto the Temple Mount. It was probably walled up by the caliphs in the seventh century, when entry to the Temple Mount was denied to all nonbelievers in Islam.

Close by the Garden of Gethsemane is the Church of the Dormition, which contains the shrine of the Tomb of the Virgin. The church is built over and around a first-century tomb which an ancient tradition maintains was temporarily the place where Mary's body lay. An anonymous work of the second or third century reports that Mary was buried in the valley of Jehoshaphat, now believed to be the Kidron valley. Another tradition, however, has it that she was buried in Ephesus. But the Byzantine emperor supported the Jerusalem tradition, and a church was built here in the late sixth century.

The rock was cut away from the tomb, following the example of the tomb in the Church of the Resurrection. To the side is another first-century tomb cut into the rock, behind a grating. It provides an example of what the original tomb had looked like before the rock was cut away. Ancient passages and walled-up entries indicated the various forms that the church, which is kept by a Greek Orthodox monk, has taken through its history.

The Franciscans, who had taken charge of the tomb in Crusader times, came into conflict with the Eastern Christian groups here and were expelled in the eighteenth century. Now, Roman Catholics honor the dormition of Mary in a large new church on Mount Zion, while the Orthodox, Armenians and Muslims venerate the traditional shrine.

The Mount of Olives: Eleona

Rising above the Garden of Gethsemane is the Eleona, the Mount of Olives, which was the site of the third great Constantinian church. The original intention of the Eleona church was to commemorate what Eusebius describes in the following words: "the feet of our Lord and Saviour . . . stood upon the Mount of Olives, by the cave which is shown there; from which, having first prayed and revealed the mysteries of the end of the world to his disciples on top of the mountain, he ascended into heaven." Eusebius refers not only to the ascension, but apparently to Christ's post-resurrection teaching during the forty days mentioned by St Luke at the beginning of Acts (1:13). The cave he mentions was probably selected as a place of prayer from very early times. Here Christians came to meditate on the several New Testament events that took place on the Mount of Olives. Beginning with the end of the fourth century, it was the custom to bury the bishops of Jerusalem at the Eleona or nearby.

One of the three grandest Byzantine churches in Palestine, Eleona was destroyed by the Persians at the very beginning of the seventh century. Today the cave and the remains of the original church are on the grounds of the Church of the Pater Noster, or Lord's Prayer, where the outlines of the old church have been reconstructed. As we faced the sanctuary, the entrance to the right led to the cave below it. Through the corridors and on the door to the cave are tiles portraying the Lord's Prayer in sixty-two languages. There has been a Carmelite Catholic convent here since the nineteenth century.

The Church of the Pater Noster is situated up the hill from the Russian convent of Gethsemane and below the summit of the mount, which is occupied by the larger Russian convent named "Eleona."

Dome of the Ascension

The site of the ascension of Jesus is a mosque, the Dome of the Ascension, situated just above the Church of the Pater Noster. Although Muslims do not accept the crucifixion of Christ, they do accept his ascension. The mosque replaces a fourth-century Byzantine church, which had been round and open to the sky in the center. Like its predecessor, the mosque is built around a rock that reputedly bears the imprint of Jesus' feet, left at the moment of the ascension. But it takes a good deal of pious imagination to discern a footprint there. The feast of the Ascension is now celebrated by Christians in the courtyard of the mosque.

The Dome of the Ascension, a Muslim site marking an event in the life of Christ, reflects the complex relations between Christians and Muslims throughout the centuries in this area, and raises the question about the place and image of Jesus in the Quran. Few Christians are aware of how deeply Muslims honor and revere Jesus. He is mentioned in almost a hundred verses of the Quran, always with reverence. The Quran recognizes that Jesus was a healer of the sick and that he raised the dead. His virgin birth, his ascension and his promised second coming are all accepted. And while the Quran ascribes many miracles to Christ, no miracles were ever claimed by Muhammad. According to Islamic believers, Muhammad's only miracle was the Quran itself—the divine book sent to the prophet to reestablish the "pure religion" that had been corrupted by unfaithful Jews and Christians.

Muslims accept Jesus as the Messiah, but it is not clear what is understood by this term in this case. Neither Muhammad nor his followers accept the Incarnation. For them, Jesus was the Word of God but not the "Son" of God, for God "did not beget, nor was he begotten," says the Quran. Muslims view the idea of the incarnation of God as incompatible with strict monotheism. Also, they generally deny that Christ was really crucified. Apparently, they regard such a death as too degrading for the greatest of the prophets before the "seal of the prophets," Muhammad. The Quran does, however, mention other righteous prophets who were killed. The rejection of the crucifixion in Islamic tradition is usually attributed to a passage in the Quran that says the Jews are reproved for saying " 'We slew the Messiah, Jesus son of Mary, the Messenger of God'—yet they did not slay him, neither crucified him, only a likeness of that was shown to them" (4:155-156). This passage is puzzling. Non-Muslims may be inclined to detect here the influence of gnosticism, which taught that Jesus, who was wholly divine, only appeared to be crucified.

Bethany

Another site that has been under Muslim protection for centuries is the Tomb of Lazarus, located in Bethany, about two miles over the Mount of Olives from the Old City. It was here that Jesus spent the nights before the celebration of the Passover, passing his days in Jerusalem during the Passion Week: "And he entered Jerusalem, and went into the temple; and when he had looked round at everything, as it was already late, he went out to Bethany with the twelve" (Mk 11:11). Bethany is open to the desert. Quite probably Christ loved its openness, which is a quality that the village has preserved. He may have come here to postpone arrest before his hour had come and to be with his village friends at the most trying period of his public ministry.

It was in Bethany that Jesus was anointed before his death:

> **And while he was at Bethany in the house of Simon the leper, as he sat at table, a woman came with an alabaster jar of ointment of pure nard, very costly, and she broke the jar and poured it over his head. But there were some who said to themselves indignantly, "Why was the ointment thus wasted? For this ointment might have been sold for more than three hundred denarii, and given to the poor." And they reproached her. But Jesus said, "Let her alone; why do you trouble her? She has done a beautiful thing to me. For you always have the poor with you, and whenever you will, you can do good to them; but you will not always have me. She has done what she could; she has anointed my body beforehand for burying. And truly, I say to you, wherever the gospel is preached in the whole world, what she has done will be told in memory of her." *(Mark 14:3-9)*

The modern name of Bethany is el-Azariyeh, the Arabic form of Lazarus. Lazarus was well known in Bethany and has been remembered throughout the centuries. Even today both Muslims and Christians venerate his tomb, which is kept by hereditary right by a Muslim family.

The story of Lazarus is given in John 11:

> Now when Jesus came, he found that Lazarus had already been in the tomb four days. Bethany was near Jerusalem, about two miles off, and many of the Jews had come to Martha and Mary to console them concerning their brother. When Martha heard that Jesus was coming, she went and met him, while Mary sat in the house. Martha said to Jesus, "Lord, if you had been here, my brother would not have died. And even now I know that whatever you ask from God, God will give you." Jesus said to her, "Your brother will rise again." Martha said to him, "I know that he will rise again in the resurrection at the last day." Jesus said to her, "I am the resurrection and the life; he who believes in me, though he die, yet shall he live, and whoever lives and believes in me shall never die. Do you believe this?" She said to him, "Yes, Lord; I believe that you are the Christ, the Son of God, he who is coming into the world." When she had said this, she went and called her sister Mary, saying quietly, "The Teacher is here and is calling for you." And when she heard it, she rose quickly and went to him. Now Jesus had not yet come to the village, but was still in the place where Martha had met him. When the Jews who were with her in the house, consoling her, saw Mary rise quickly and go out, they followed her, supposing that she was going to the tomb to weep there. Then Mary, when she came where Jesus was and saw him, fell at his feet, saying to him, "Lord, if you had been here, my brother would not have died." When Jesus saw her weeping, and the Jews who came with her also weeping, he was deeply moved in spirit and troubled; and he said, "Where have you laid him?" They said to him, "Lord, come and see." Jesus wept. So the Jews said, "See how he loved him!" But some of them said, "Could not he who opened the eyes of the blind man have kept this man from dying?"

> The Jesus, deeply moved again, came to the tomb; it was a cave, and a stone lay upon it. Jesus said, "Take away the stone." Martha, the sister of the dead man, said to him, "Lord, by this time there will be an odor, for he has been dead four days." Jesus said to her, "Did I not tell you that if you would believe you would see the glory of God?" So they took away the stone. And Jesus lifted up his eyes and said, "Father, I thank thee that thou hast heard me. I knew that thou hearest me always, but I have said this on account of the people standing by, that they may believe that thou didst sent me."

When he had said this, he cried with a loud voice, "Lazarus, come out." The dead man came out, his hands and feet bound with bandages, and his face wrapped with a cloth. Jesus said to them, "Unbind him, and let him go." *(John 11:17-44)*

To enter the tomb one must descend a very steep flight of stone steps. After a mosque had been built over the site, the original entrance to the tomb was closed to Christians, so the present entrance was carved through the rock. Entrance to the tomb itself is achieved by backing down, as on the ladder of a ship. The Russian Synodal Church celebrates here on Lazarus Saturday, liturgically reliving each year the events described in the Gospel of John. The clergy and procession must back down also into the tomb, which is so small that only a few persons can stand in it. The location may well be authentic, although the appearance and structures associated with it have changed through the centuries.

Russian Sites

The Russian presence in Palestine became important in numbers and wealth in the nineteenth century, when thousands of pilgrims from Russia poured into the Holy Land each year. The Russian compound to the west of the old city, built to house them, was the first structure erected outside the old city walls. The Russians showed particular concern for the well-being of the local Orthodox Christians. By 1907, more than eighty schools for Arab Christians had been founded with Russian funds in Palestine, and ten thousand students were receiving instruction in their native tongue and in Russian, with many of them going on to Russia for professional training. The Russians built and restored churches, and were among the first archeologists.

All this work and money broke off abruptly after the 1917 Revolution. Under the British Mandate and the Kingdom of Jordan, Russian properties were administered by the Russian Synodal Church in Exile. Then in 1948, the new Israeli government handed over the compound to the west of the old city as well as most of the rent-producing properties to the Patriarchal Church in the Soviet Union. The properties under the control of Jordan—including the convents at Gethsemane and on the Mount of Olives and the monastery at Hebron—remained in Synodal hands. When Israel entered this territory in 1967, the political situation had changed drastically, and the Israeli government no longer wished to support a Moscow-backed church.

School at Bethany

An Arab School for Girls in Bethany is still under the auspices of the Russian Synodal Church. The school has a curious history. In the early part of this century, a Scottish noblewoman discovered the Russian Orthodox Church in Palestine, joined it, and decided to use all her resources to serve the Christian Arab children of Bethany. She then helped build this school on the site traditionally associated with the meeting of Mary and Martha with Jesus outside the town, when the two sisters told the Lord that their brother Lazarus was dead. The school was opened in 1934, with new and modern equipment and a modern educational philosophy. Today most of the teachers are Arab, and the bulk of their salaries comes from Jordan. Some fixed sums come from foundations in England and the United States. The alert, affectionate and enthusiastic headmistress is Mother Sophia, a Russian nun over seventy who spent her youth in Czechoslovakia and Paris.

The Russian churches and communities, with their architecture, icons and music, still maintain a rich spiritual tradition. They have shown admirable tenaciousness and devotion to surmount the obstacles raised by time and history.

Church of Mary Magdalene

In striking contrast to its surroundings, St Mary Magdalene in Gethsemane lifts its gold onion domes above the surrounding olive trees and cypresses in the Garden of Gethsemane. It was built in 1888 by Tsar Alexander III. The handsome grounds of the monastery within the walled compound contain a part of the ancient set of steps leading up the hill and over the Mount of Olives. It is virtually certain that Jesus passed this way as he went back and forth from Bethany to Jerusalem during the Passion Week.

Within the church, above the altar, is a huge fresco designed by a well-known Russian painter of the time, Vereshchagin, depicting the legend of

Mary Magdalene offering a red egg to a Roman official. The style and theme of this painting seems already dated. A far older, smaller icon by the entrance portrays Mary Magdalene as she recognized the risen Christ. This is the true icon of Mary Magdalene.

The Russian nuns of Gethsemane wear a distinctive high headdress and the beautiful singing of their choir is widely known. They are aging and dwindling in number. Some younger Arab Christians have joined their community. In the congregation there are occasional Russian converts who have recently emigrated from the Soviet Union to Israel. Diminished resources and changing social and political conditions seem to threaten the continuation of the monastery in its present form.

In the crypt of the monastery in Gethsemane are the remains of the Grand Duchess Elizabeth Fedorovna. The sister of the last tsarina, Alexandra, and widow of the Grand Duke Sergius, she had been active in the Russian mission to Jerusalem, became a nun, and then was murdered by the revolutionaries in 1918. Her body was somehow transported east to Harbin, China, and in 1921, was conveyed by ship to Jerusalem, where she had wished to be buried. She and her companion, Sister Barbara, were subsequently recognized as saints, being canonized together with the New Russian Martyrs by the Russian Synodal Church in November 1981. The relics, the only ones of the new martyrs outside the borders of the Soviet Union, were transferred to the main church in May 1982.

Eleona Convent

Another important Russian Orthodox landmark in Jerusalem is Eleona, the convent with large grounds on top of the Mount of Olives. Most of the structures on the grounds, including the main church and the bell tower, were built in the nineteenth century, from 1870 to 1877. The tall tower has long been the highest structure in Jerusalem and is a landmark of the city's skyline, visible for many miles around. The oldest building is the Church of St John the Baptist. According to one tradition, John's head was buried here, and this Byzantine church was built to commemorate it. A mosaic floor, with striking plants and animals and an Armenian inscription, recalls the Armenian floor in the mortuary chapel near the Damascus Gate.

From the monastery walls there are remarkable views, with the city off to one direction and the desert off to the other. It is often possible to see as far as the Dead Sea from here. Russian pilgrims come here from all over the world and stay either in the monastery itself or in a nearby hotel.

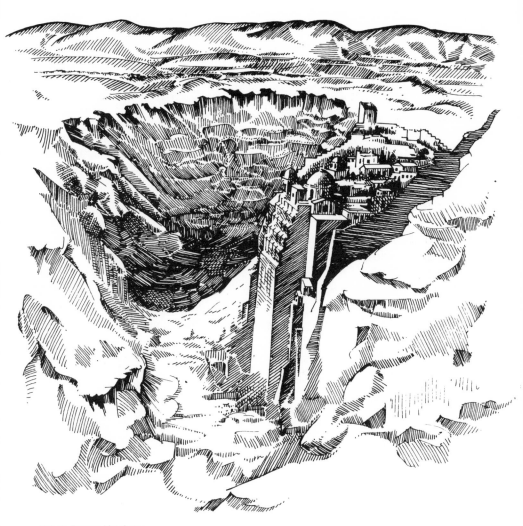

Judean Desert: Mar Saba,
5th century monastery

THE JUDEAN DESERT

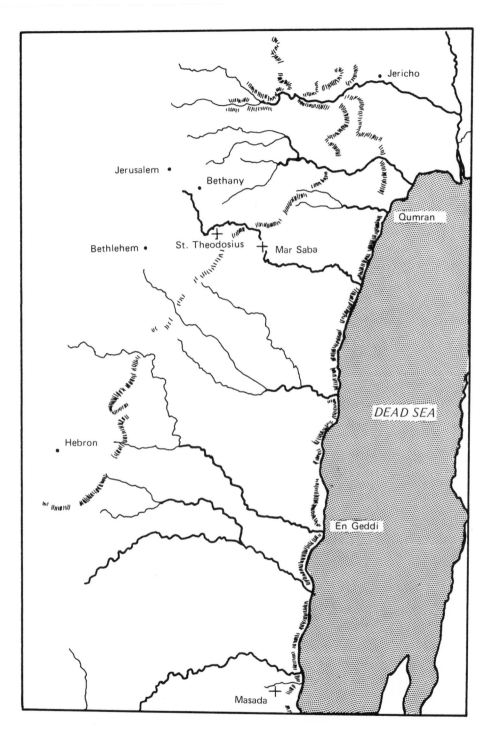

THE DESERT AND THE DEAD SEA

The City and the Desert

The Judean desert presents formidable physical challenges as well as spiritual riches. The city of Jerusalem confronts the desert. On the west side of the Mount of Olives lies Jerusalem, and on the east stretches the desert. The contrast between the city and the Judean desert dominates the geography of the southern part of Israel, or Judea. The Mount of Olives appears as the dividing line between the city, which has been destroyed and rebuilt time and again throughout the centuries, and the desert, which remains without change. At the same time, the Mount of Olives is the link that brings them together, standing as a visible and majestic symbol of "eternity" entering "time"—where the desert invades the city and where the separation between them seems impossible to maintain. Driving through the desert, one can spot the belltower at Eleona on the top of the Mount of Olives at many points. This physical, geographical landmark also serves as a spiritual point of orientation.

Both the city and the desert have their particular attractive and distinctive characteristics. Anyone who has seen Jerusalem from the Mount of Olives will forever keep the image of this unique city, with its hills and valleys and above all its holy places, which have captivated Jews, Christians and Muslims for hundreds of years.

In the city we are conscious of ourselves, and of the divisions and dangers in city life. The desert is different. In the desert we are more aware of others, of those who have lived and still live there. Lesley Hazleton, an Israeli journalist born and educated in England, writes in her book *Where Mountains Roar* that "the desert can take us beyond what we think of ourselves into another wider order of being." It is a world that offers "a simplicity of being." Yet this experience does not come easily—the desert too has its dangers to life and health. In biblical history, the desert is a place of God's revelation and of human temptation. Jesus was alone "with wild beasts" in the wilderness (or desert)—it was there that he was tempted and had to overcome the devil.

The wilderness or desert of Judea is not at all a smooth or even sandy stretch of land. It is full of hills without greenery and valleys without water. One hill throws its shadow on another, making for a vast display of different shades of sandy brown colors. Thus, it has its own particular diversity, against a background of undifferentiated wilderness.

For anyone driving through the Judean wilderness—from Jerusalem to Masada and Qumran or to the Mar Saba Monastery—it is easy to understand why the wilderness has served so well as a refuge for fugitives, why David could escape from Saul's pursuit there, and why ancient and modern hermits have chosen it as a place of prayer and meditation. Those who are familiar with the desert know that the hills and valleys are not alike, but for one who is lost—and it is easy to be lost there—all are just the same. There are no natural points of orientation in the desert.

When Christ was praying at Gethsemane "Abba, Father, all things are possible to thee; remove this cup from me; yet not what I will, but what thou wilt" (Mark 14:36), he was not far from the Judean desert. In about fifteen minutes he could have walked into the desert, and neither Judas nor anyone else would have been able to find him.

The Christian hermits who populated the desert in Byzantine times were not trying to separate themselves from others or to seek only their own redemption. They sought solitude in order to help all those whom they left behind in their native cities and villages. Jacques Valentin once remarked to a monk he met on Mount Athos, "But what surprises me is that you, detached from the world as you are, are still so close to us. When we talk to you, you might be in close touch with other men."

To think that monks go into the desert to forget others or to isolate themselves for selfish reasons is to misunderstand what they are about. They surely do not withdraw there out of self-interest. Who would go into the wilderness, exposing himself to its hardships and dangers, for selfish reasons? As psychologists have observed, the selfish man is incapable of even loving himself, or of making a sacrifice even for himself. The life of a hermit is a life of obedience and renunciation, which is diametrically opposed to selfishness.

The monks went out to the solitude of the desert in order to become explorers for others, searchers in a realm that others are unable to visit, in the words of a modern monk, Thomas Merton. They came to the wilderness to examine and explore a desert area of man's heart—for in the desert theories are of no help, and one learns that only experience can be relied on. This pursuit of a life of solitude is motivated by love for God and desire for the experience of God, of his transcendence, power and mercy.

The Dead Sea Area

The road from Jerusalem to the Dead Sea leads through the Judean desert. Along the way, the vegetation becomes more and more scant. At first patches of green indicate where quick-growing wheat is cultivated, then all growth stops. The rugged landscape turns dirt brown, showing patterns formed by erosion and runoffs—the land will not hold water. The air becomes oppressive and hot.

Just before the Dead Sea the road descends quite sharply. This sea, about fifty miles in length, is the lowest point on earth. It lies still and baking in the tropical sun, with white mineral deposits from evaporation along the shore. At the southern part of the Sea, just above the area of ancient Sodom, potash works have been in operation for some time, providing much of the world's supply of this vital mineral. Turning north, the road runs between the brown forbidding cliffs and the equally forbidding lifeless sea, furnishing dramatic views and an eerie light and atmosphere. At its narrowest point it is almost possible to ford the sea to the east side, which is the territory of Jordan. The level of the sea is falling, although not consistently. There is a plan to bring water in from the Mediterranean, which would allow the development of hydroelectric power because of the sharp drop in altitude between the two seas. The outsider cannot help wondering what the effect of the Mediterranean water would be on the properties of the Dead Sea and the general ecology of the region. Despite the harsh climate, there are popular health spas at En Geddi and at other points along the western shore of the Dead Sea.

Masada

Masada, an enormous rock about half a mile long, is the most spectacular place in the country and still a potent historical symbol. Located a third of the way up the west shore of the sea, it was the last stronghold captured in the Roman-Jewish War, finally falling in 73 A.D.

Josephus, in the first century, described Masada as "a rock with a very large perimeter and lofty all the way along is on every side broken off by deep ravines. Their bottom is out of sight, and from it rise sheer cliffs on which no animal can get a foot-hold except in two places, where the rock can with great difficulty be climbed." On this rock the high priest Jonathan (152-143 B.C.) built a fortress, which he named Masada, "mountain stronghold." Later, Herod the Great refortified it and built a palace on the western slope. Josephus notes that Herod placed particular importance on this fortress, as a refuge for himself in the event that the Jewish masses forced him from his throne, or in case the Egyptian Queen Cleopatra, with the help of the Romans, succeeded in removing him and in bringing the Kingdom of Judea under her own rule.

At the beginning of the first Jewish War (A.D. 66), the Zealots and the Sicarii—a group of extreme Jewish nationalists who used *sicae* (short daggers) to systematically assassinate their political opponents—established themselves on Masada under the leadership of Eleazar, and were able to maintain their position until the year 73. Josephus gives us a vivid and dramatic account of the Roman siege, Masada's defense and the mass suicide of the defenders that took place that year. When the defenders saw that defeat was inevitable, Eleazar collected the toughest of his comrades and urged them to slay first the members of their own families and then one another. "Let our wives die unabused, our children without knowledge of slavery; after that, let us do each other an ungrudging kindness, preserving our freedom as a glorious winding-sheet. But first let our possessions and the whole fortress go up in flames; it will be a bitter blow to the Romans, that I know, to find our persons beyond their reach and nothing left for them to loot. One thing only let us spare—our store of food; it will bear witness when we are dead to the fact that we perished, not through want but because, as we resolved at the beginning, we chose death rather than slavery."

With their death Eleazar wanted to deny the Romans "their hoped-for pleasure at our expense" and to leave them dumbfounded by death and awed by the courage of Masada's defenders. And at dawn, when the Romans, expecting desperate resistance, made their final assault, they were met by a dreadful silence. They gave a shout, expecting someone from inside to appear. But only two women, who with five children had escaped the slaying, emerged from their hiding place to give the Romans a detailed account of what had taken place: how the seventy rebels and their families committed suicide rather than yield to Roman power.

On all sides of Masada are extremely steep cliffs. However, when you reach the top (presumably by cable car) and look around from its center, the edges of the rock disappear, blending in with the hills around it. You have the illusion that you are on the same stretch of land as the desert that surrounds you on three sides, with the Dead Sea to the east.

At one end of the rock was Herod's fort, and his palace was at the other. At the palace, archeologists have uncovered the remains of the most spectacular of all of Herod's building projects. In what must have been a real challenge to

Masada

the builders, a grand palace with three levels was constructed in this hostile climate and impossibly high location. Remains of cisterns and water pipes indicate careful planning; they were vital for the security of the palace. There were also elegant Roman-style baths, which were not Jewish ritual baths. Herod, the "king of the Jews," cared little for Jewish customs, and when he built these baths he was copying Hellenistic Roman practices. From the baths, steep, modern stairways lead down to the intermediate and then the lower level of the palace. Here frescoes are preserved under glass amid elegant Greek pillars. It was truly a pleasure palace in this forbidding site, though it was in use only a short time.

Near the palace two sets of facing seats have been excavated, identified as a synagogue, but scholars doubt that it was part of the original palace of Herod. Herod, who erected temples at Sebaste and Caesarea to Augustus to please the emperor, had no religious commitment to Judaism. The synagogue found in his palace at Masada was probably added by the Jewish Zealots some seventy years after his death. But whoever built it, this synagogue, oriented toward Jerusalem, would seem to be the oldest one extant.

After the archeologist Yigael Yadin had uncovered what he thought to be a synagogue on Masada, he invited some heads of the Jewish religious groups in Israel to come to see it. When they told him that they would like to pray there, he warned them that he could not be completely certain that it had been a synagogue. The rabbis responded, "From now on it is."

The Monastery of Euthymius

As we have seen, the Byzantines built abundantly and richly during their tenure in Palestine. Anywhere you go, from Galilee to Judea and beyond, you find the ruins and mosaics of splendid Byzantine churches and monasteries. And the Byzantine monks reached the top of Masada as well.

The monastery on Masada was built by St Euthymius, who came to Jerusalem from Melitene, on the Euphrates River, in the early fifth century. He had been ordained at a young age, and his abilities soon led to offers of promotion to positions of authority in the Church. To avoid such renown, he fled from his native land and came to Jerusalem. Later, fearing that he might be called to a position of power in the holy city, he and another monk left the city and set up a church on the very top of Masada. But he did not stay long on Masada, moving on to establish another monastery in Hebron.

Euthymius and his monks used the stones from the ruins of Herod's structures to build their monastery and church. The church, which was oriented toward the east, rather than Jerusalem, as churches traditionally were, contains mosaics on the floor and carefully executed stonework on the walls. But after all the labor it must have taken to build this monastery, it apparently proved too difficult to keep the monks in this unfavorable location, and the monastery was abandoned.

Qumran: The Essene Community

About an hour's drive north from Masada lies Qumran, the Essene monastic community where the Dead Sea Scrolls were discovered. This community of Jewish hermits settled here around 140 B.C. They suffered from a severe earthquake in 31 B.C., when some thirty thousand Judeans perished. During the reign of Herod's son and successor Archelaus (4 B.C.-A.D. 6) the community started rebuilding their old settlement, which was finally destroyed by the Romans at the time of the first-century Roman-Jewish war. Before the Romans razed the settlement, however, the sectarians succeeded in hiding their scrolls in caves in the surrounding desert, where Bedouin shepherds discovered them in 1947. Some of the Essenes, it seems, escaped from Qumran to Masada, for their scrolls were found there as well.

The monks of Qumran are known to us as Essenes. We do not know for sure the origin of this name, but it is usually assumed that the designation is derived from *hasya* (pl. *hasen*), which is the Aramaic of the Hebrew word *hasid*, "pious one." The Essenes' history goes back to the second-century sect of the Hasideans or Hasidim, which strongly supported the Maccabean revolt of 165 B.C. against Hellenization. (The term "Judaism" first appears in 2 Maccabees, which was written in the second century, and is used to describe the Jewish way of life in contrast to Hellenism.) The "pious ones" saw the greatest danger to Judaism in the attempts of the Seleucid king Antiochus IV Epiphanes to expand his policy of Hellenization into the Temple itself. The king, who claimed that Zeus was manifested in his person, had even gone so far as to set up an altar to the Olympian Zeus in the Temple.

The revolt proved successful, but the victory brought division among the Hasideans, some of whom now broke with the ruling Maccabees over their new policies. One source of the rupture was the Maccabean leader Jonathan's acceptance, in 152 B.C., of the office of high priest. As Jonathan was not a member of the official Zadokite line of succession to the high priesthood, this act signified, to the Essenes, a break with the traditional Hebrew priestly line, and from then on the Essenes would have no further dealings with the Jerusalem hierarchy.

The Essenes also disagreed with other policies and innovations in Jerusalem, such as the introduction of the lunar calendar in the worship in the Temple, replacing the old solar calendar. Their deep concern for the calendar caused some historians of the movement to characterize them as "calendar specialists." The solar calendar they wished to preserve is a fixed calendar—Passover, for instance, falls on the same weekday every year. One could not follow the way of the Essenes without following their calendar. This issue is important to take into account when discussing the relationship of Jesus and the Essenes. From what we know from the gospels, Jesus followed the calendar of the Temple in Jerusalem.

Having rejected the leadership of Jerusalem, the Essenes built their city in the desert at Qumran and followed the Teacher of Righteousness or the Righteous Teacher. This Righteous Teacher appears as the leader of the new sectarian group either at the end of the Maccabean leader Jonathan's reign (160-142) or at the beginning of the reign of Simon (142-134), who, by agreement of the rest of the Jewish people and priests, would head the legitimate line of the high priesthood "until a true prophet should appear" (1 Maccabees

14:41). The Righteous Teacher was probably a priest of the Zadokite line who shared the views of the Hasideans. According to the Qumran document, he was persecuted by the Wicked Priest (either Jonathan or Simon) and forced to flee into the wilderness. At Qumran, however, he was respected and admired as the true teacher and interpreter of the law. Yet this Righteous Teacher never claimed to be the Messiah. Together with the Essene community, he himself was awaiting the coming of a messianic priest of Aaron's line and a messianic king of David's.

In the second century B.C. there were about two hundred Essenes living in Qumran. Were the Essenes married or not? Philo of Alexandria (ca. 25 B.C.-50 A.D.), a Jewish philosopher, tells us that they were a celibate group in the desert. Josephus, the first century Jewish historian, writes that some Essenes "neglect wedlock, but choose out other persons' children while they are pliable and fit for learning . . . and form them according to their own manners." But, he adds, "there is another order of Essenes, who agree with the rest as to their way of living and customs and laws, but differ from them in the point of marriage, as thinking that by not marrying they cut off the principal part of human life, which is the prospect of succession . . . that if all men should be of the same opinion . . . the whole race of mankind would fail."

A main burial ground with skeletons of adult males has been excavated, as has another with female skeletons. The Qumran evidence suggests that some Essenes were married, but that the greater number of them was celibate. It is possible that at the very beginning, when the community was founded, all were celibate. Later the leaders allowed a mixed congregation of celibate and non-celibate Essenes. It has also been argued that from the very beginning married Essenes coexisted with a much larger group of celibates. Whatever the case may be, there is unmistakable archeological evidence that the skeletons of women and children have been discovered at Qumran. These may be of later date than the male skeletons; if so this would suggest that all the Essenes during the founding period were unmarried males.

The Dead Sea Scrolls

The documents discovered in the cave at Qumran contain parts of almost every book of the Old Testament, as well as a number of writings related to the life and discipline of the community. Their chief importance lies in providing us with a text of the Old Testament that is much earlier than any we possessed before 1947. Textual critics are using the Qumran documents to establish a

Fragments from the Dead Sea Scrolls, discovered in Qumran, near the Dead Sea.

pre-Christian text of the Hebrew scriptures. The scrolls also provide valuable data attesting to the diversity in early Judaism and the atmosphere before the destruction of the Temple in A.D. 68-70.

Moreover, the documents provide valuable background material for understanding the New Testament period. In particular, they supply us with the basis of the theological language used most extensively in the Gospel of St John. Before the writings of the Essenes were found, many scholars believed that the fourth evangelist was under strong Hellenistic influence when he wrote his gospel, but because of the language we find in the Qumran scrolls, this theory has been dropped. Words and images such as truth, knowledge, light and darkness were once thought to belong outside the world of Palestinian Judaism, and thus the Gospel of John was considered by critics to be the "most Hellenistic" of the four. Now it is recognized as the "most Jewish," incorporating historical material preserved and transmitted in a Jewish, Aramaic-speaking environment.

Although the language of the Dead Sea Scrolls sheds important light on the New Testament scriptures, the documents also prove that the Essenes had no effect on the doctrines of primitive Christianity. In the desert, the Essenes devoted themselves to keeping and living under the law, and were eagerly awaiting the anointed ones of Yahweh. The words of Isaiah—"Behold, I send my messenger before thy face, who shall prepare thy way; the voice of one crying in the wilderness: Prepare the way of the Lord, make his paths straight"

(40:3)—were applied by the community to itself. John the Baptist disagreed with them, applying these words to his own role as the herald of the Messiah, Jesus Christ (Mark 1:2-3). The Essenes, according to the testimony of Josephus, believed that bodies are corruptible but that souls are immortal. Souls continue forever and are united to their bodies as to prisons "into which they are drawn by a certain natural enticement, but when they are set free from the bonds of the flesh, they then, as released from a long bondage, rejoice and mount upward." This belief, perhaps affected by Hellenistic thought, was in sharp contrast to the traditional Jewish attitude toward the body, as well as to Christian doctrine. When the Christian monks erected their cities in the desert, they believed in a messiah who had already come; they lived by the power of his resurrection, and they awaited the final transformation of all things, including the body.

The very setting of the community, between the Dead Sea and the caves of the desert, is most impressive. Excavations are still being carried out on this spot. Prominent among the discoveries are the cisterns, essential for preserving life in this stark, uninviting environment. Archeologists have also identified scriptoria, refectories and meeting rooms, but no living quarters. It is assumed that the monks lived in caves or temporary shelters and came to the center for communal activities. From the wall around the excavations one can see the cave where some of the Dead Sea Scrolls were found.

Desert Oases

Jericho: An Oasis

Setting off to the north again, to the end of the sea where the Jordan flows in, and then over the desert hills beyond, one comes suddenly upon palms and fruit trees, flowers and houses. This is the oasis of Jericho, one of the most ancient inhabited places in the world. Outside the town is a large compound of mud huts, now uninhabited, where Palestinian refugees had lived from 1948 until 1967, when they fled elsewhere.

Beyond Jericho in fenced excavations is the oldest city archeologists have ever found, dating back to 7000 B.C. The old wall turned out to be part of a fortress, defense being man's earliest community need. This section had been excavated by Kathleen Kenyon, whose find was particularly noteworthy because so many other archeologists had been working in that area before her, but she proved able to interpret what they all had missed.

Above the tell, on the brown hills beyond the city, stands the Greek monastery at Quruntel, built on what is traditionally considered the site of Jesus' forty days of temptation in the wilderness. There are a few monks living there at present.

Mar Saba Monastery: A Spiritual Oasis

Mar Saba, one of the oldest continuously occupied Christian monasteries, is situated about fifteen miles from Jerusalem, in the Judean desert east of Bethlehem. It is on a steep hillside in the Kidron gorge. For most of the way there is a paved road, but then a stony dirt road winds from one Bedouin settlement to another in the desert.

Most of Israel's Bedouins live in the northern part of the Negev. Their approach to the desert is very different from that of people in western nations. Instead of altering the environment and taming the wilderness, the Bedouin accept it as it is; they admit that the desert is stronger than themselves. For them the desert is a fact of life that cannot be removed or changed. The desert also inculcates fatalism: like death, the desert is always there.

Because of the monastery's position in the Kidron gorge, it is not possible to catch sight of its buildings until one is right over them. All around is the desert, with the monastic city and its attractive colors standing in its midst—a spiritual oasis in the midst of barrenness. Monks have been praying here almost without interruption since the end of the fifth century, serving God and proclaiming Christ's victory over death and the powers of darkness.

The monastery is named after its founder, the great spiritual leader St Saba (439-532). He had come to the Holy Land from Cappadocia around 456, and first received spiritual direction from St Euthymius (who, as we noted earlier, was the founder of the monastery on Masada). Euthymius sent the still beardless young monk to another spiritual leader, the Abbot Theoctistas (d. 466), for further monastic training in the latter's cenobitic monastery, where for a long period the future saint took care of the donkeys. Before setting up his own monastery in the desert, he lived for a full five years in a cave to which the only access was by climbing a rope attached to the entrance. The only water was in a cistern a mile and a half away. Here in the cave he acquired clarity of vision, cleansed the image of God in which he was created, fought the spirit of temptation, came into contact with the wild beasts of the wilderness, prayed to God and meditated on his glory, mercy and goodness. He came to know that God was not only somewhere "above there" but near and in the human person. And in the desert God fought alongside St Saba—for Saba knew that without God's help he could not win any spiritual battles.

After these experiences, he built his monastery, in 482. The Mar Saba Monastery has endured through the centuries up to the present time, its saints giving hope to many, defending the faith in times of controversy and bearing witness to Christ in times of persecution.

From the foot of the "Women's Tower," or the Tower of St Simeon, the whole monastery spreads out below, with the blue domes of the churches and the stepped ruins climbing the hills across the way. The only sounds are the twittering of birds and the constant running water, a strange sound in the desert. Actually the water is unusable, being filled with sewage from Jerusalem running down the Kidron. The monks have to collect water for themselves in cisterns during the winter rains.

Only men may enter the monastery itself. Once inside the gate, the visitor descends to the lower level of the monastery, where the tomb of St Saba originally lay. The body of the saint now lies in the main chapel, the Chapel of the Annunciation, in a coffin with a glass cover. The Crusaders had removed Saba's body from its original resting place and had taken it to Bari in Italy. It was only in 1965 that Pope Paul VI, to improve relations between the churches, returned the relics to the monastery that the saint had built. The relics are well preserved.

Almost all the objects in the principal chapel, including the icons, are from the nineteenth century. An earthquake in 1834 had severely damaged the monastery, and after that it needed a thorough reconstruction, new ornaments and liturgical items to replace what had been lost. However, the Chapel of St Nicholas, located in the cave of the original church, has an iconostasis containing royal doors that date from the fifteenth century, and several icons on the walls date from this time as well. This lower chapel has a rock ceiling, and on each side of the altar are skulls of monks who were murdered by the Persians in the year 614.

When the monks of Mar Saba were informed of the terrible tortures that might befall them with the coming of the Persians, the abbot and most of the monks fled into the Arabian desert. But forty-four monks chose to remain in the monastery, to be tortured when they refused to reveal the secret places where the monastery's treasures were hidden, and eventually murdered. Their skulls are more than just a reminder of the horror and destruction perpetuated by the Persians in 614, about twenty-five years before the arrival of the Arabs in Palestine. They are "martyrs," witnesses to the faith.

There is a story that just before his death St Saba told his monks that in some distant future another "Saba," from a western country, would come to visit the monastery. When he came, he was to be given St Saba's own staff and two icons of the Theotokos. Seven hundred years later, in 1229 and 1234, St Sava, the head of the autocephalous Serbian Church, made two pilgrimages to the Holy Land. During his first pilgrimage he stayed in the Mar Saba Monastery and left many gifts. He also studied the life of the monks and their Typikon. Saba himself had been responsible for the compilation of prayers and services that became known as the Jerusalem Typikon, which has been in use in all Orthodox churches throughout the centuries. The differences we now find in the services and practices of local Orthodox churches are of relatively recent date and reflect various national customs. Today, as in the past, all Orthodox in principle recognize St Saba's Typikon.

At the end of his stay at the monastery, St Sava received what the founder of the monastery had left for him more than seven hundred years before, and returned to Mount Athos with the two icons and the staff. One of these two icons is known as the "Three-handed Theotokos," and it is linked with St John of Damascus (d. 776), who lived in Mar Saba. John was a great defender of the veneration of icons during the iconoclast controversy, and to punish him the iconoclast emperor had ordered one of his arms cut off. The saint then prayed to the Theotokos, who healed him, and in gratitude he added a third arm of silver to an icon of the Theotokos. This icon is now the most venerated icon in Hilander, the Serbian monastery on Mount Athos, although the icon we see there today is possibly a fourteenth-century copy of its legendary prototype. The other icon given to St Sava is also still on Mount Athos, in Sava's "House of Silence" at Karyes, the capital of the monastic state. And the staff remains at Athos in a little cell called the Pateritza, which means "pastoral staff."

After a steep climb the visitor reaches a chapel containing the tomb of St John of Damascus. His body however was removed by the Crusaders, whom a Russian nun we met characterized as "pious and ungodly barbarians." No one is certain where it is now. From this chapel a few steps lead down to the cell where St John wrote and prayed. Beside his defense of icons, St John of Damascus was also known for his summation of patristic theology and for hymnography. The Christian world would have been much poorer, artistically and theologically, without his work.

Next to the Chapel of Sts Joachim and Anna is the cell of St Saba. Immediately noticeable is a large fresco of the saint with a lion. One day while St Saba was resting, a lion came into his cell and pulled at the edge of his garment, not hard but enough to catch the saint's attention. Saba looked at the lion without fear and continued his silent prayer. Then the lion left. The next day the lion reappeared and pulled his garment much harder. This time the saint turned toward the lion and said: "Listen, in this cell there is enough space for both of us. If you would like to share it with me, stay, and let us live together. But if you do not want to do this, then you should leave me and go somewhere else." The lion looked intensely at him for a few moments, but in the end decided to leave the cell, never to return.

Christ was alone with wild beasts during his temptation, and there are many accounts of saints who had special relations with the animal world. They all point to the harmony that Christ restored between man and the animal kingdom that had existed before the Fall.

St Saba's cell contains a hole in its rocky walls, called the *hesychastirion*, where the saint used to seclude himself in silent prayer undisturbed by anyone, including the lion. It was a very small space, with no room to stand or sit properly. To pray there, one would have to assume a crouching position, as Saba did in his long hours of vigil.

At present there are fewer than ten monks in this large monastic city. A pilgrim today in these underpopulated monasteries will find few "holy men" to show them the holy places. Yet those who manage to visit the monasteries will find them rich centers of the historical, artistic and spiritual tradition of the church. Even if they are not attracted to a prolonged stay in these desert shrines, they will recognize that in the early history of the church it was those who lived in the wilderness that kept those in the cities spiritually alive.

Entrance, Mar Saba

It was different in the fourth century when Egeria visited several monastic establishments. Describing her visit to Mount Sinai, she writes that, after receiving communion, at the conclusion of the service, "at once I asked (the monks) if they would point out to us all the different places. The holy men willingly agreed . . . They showed us all the other places we wanted to see, and also the ones they knew about themselves." At Edessa in Mesopotamia "the holy bishop of the city" welcomed her and said, "My daughter, I can see what a long journey this is on which your faith has brought you—right from the other end of the earth. So now please let us show you all the places Christians should visit here." And Egeria added that she gave thanks to God and eagerly accepted the bishop's invitation. The bishop "was at pains to show us all there was to see."

The monks of Mar Saba have always been spiritually strengthened by their proximity to the holy places in Jerusalem, on the Mount of Olives and in Bethlehem. The churches of the Nativity in Bethlehem, the Holy Resurrection in Jerusalem and the Ascension on the Mount of Olives continue to hold generations of monks to the roots of the Christian faith and to its historical founder, Jesus Christ. These sacred sites continually remind them of the way of life and the perfection of the gospel. For without the distinct Christian doctrines of the incarnation, resurrection and ascension, Christianity, together with its monasticism, could not have survived the onslaughts of Islam. Many ancient fortresses collapsed because in the end there were not enough people to use and defend them. But Mar Saba stood as an indestructible spiritual fortress of the faith.

Derwas J. Chitty, in his book *The Desert City*, conveys to us the importance and influence of the Mar Saba monastery for the Christian world in general and for the Palestinian Christians in particular. The power of the holy places kept these Christians to "a sober historical faith," and "those who have heard, after thirteen centuries, the bell of Mar Saba clanging out at night over the wilderness, have recognized there, in spite of all vicissitudes and shortcomings of man who still needs his Saviour, the abiding triumph of Easter."

Those who practice a rigorous discipline of prayer are particularly aware of the importance of certain places for their spiritual endeavors. A spiritual father on Mount Athos once told the young French visitor Jacques Valentin: "We hermits gather here, on this cliff, because Karoulia is a privileged place. When I am at prayer in my chapel, I am helped by the souls of all those who have lived here throughout the centuries. Any monk on Mount Athos will tell you the same thing: when we are walking the paths of the peninsula and praying, there are certain places where our concentration and our fervour always come more easily and better. The state of grace always occurs at places where for centuries monks have stopped to rest and meditate: the divine presence is felt more strongly in these places than elsewhere."

Afterword: The Holy Land and Modern Society

The Place of Christian Pilgrimage

The sacred places in Jerusalem and elsewhere in the Holy Land are uniquely privileged. They have been sanctified by the presence of Christ himself, by his words, works, life, death and resurrection. Prayer at these places rises spontaneously, concentration is effortless, and meditation comes naturally.

Today one sees pilgrims from many nations coming in a steady stream to sites that are sacred to them. Many of them come with Bibles open, to relive the events described and to transcend the limitations of their own time. Here it is easy to agree with an Ukrainian widow who became a nun in Eleona: "Sometimes I feel dissatisfied here and think of going away. But then I say to myself: How could you think of leaving these holy places? and I cry and ask the Lord to forgive me for such thoughts. When I first came I was weeping tears of joy all the time I was here." Her blue eyes filled again with tears as she spoke. Another nun, a school principal, put these sentiments in quite a different context: "We must know Christian history to keep a spiritual balance," she observed, stressing the healthy influence of the holy places on those who visit them and live among them. Attraction to them and awareness of their importance have brought pilgrims to these sites since the founding of the Church.

What is the place of pilgrimage in the Christian faith? In the early patristic period, when pilgrimages to the Holy Land began on a large scale, Christian leaders and theologians were not unanimous in their opinions of the importance and value of visits to the sacred sites of the Holy Land. Some enthusiastically encouraged Christians to visit these places; others discouraged them, warning of the dangers involved in traveling and in staying in the city, with its corrupt style of life.

Eusebius of Caesarea was among the first to encourage pilgrimages to Jerusalem. He regarded the tomb of Christ, the holy cave, as visible testimony to the resurrection of Christ. To him, no voice could bear as clear a witness to Christ's victory over death as the site of that victory itself.

St Cyril, the fourth-century bishop of Jerusalem, also stressed the witness of the New Testament places to the events that took place in them. In a catechetical lecture in the Martyrium, which was built over the site of the crucifixion, he linked the holy places with other witnesses, divine and human. As the Father testified to his Son from heaven and the Holy Spirit bore witness by descending in the form of a dove, and as John the Baptist and many prophets before him affirmed that Jesus is the Messiah, so the places linked with Jesus' name themselves do the same. "This Golgotha, sacred above all such places, bears witness by its very look. The most holy tomb bears witness," as also do the Mount of Olives and Gethsemane, and "there are many more besides," Cyril concludes.

Among Cyril's contemporaries, St Gregory of Nyssa took an opposing view. He visited Jerusalem around 380. In a letter entitled "On Pilgrimages," addressed to a monk in his native Cappadocia, Gregory described his visit and expressed his disappointment with life in Jerusalem. His attitude may be explained in part by the fact that he had been sent there to bring peace among the quarreling clergy. He writes that all was in confusion "with the heads of the holy Jerusalem churches and (they) needed an arbiter." The fact that the Christian leaders in the city where the Lord was crucified and resurrected were so passionately involved in personal disputes profoundly disturbed him. Sin, he declared, is a way of life among those who live in Jerusalem. "Well, in a place where such things go on, what proof, I ask, have you of the abundance of Divine Grace?"

St Gregory discouraged pilgrimages to Jerusalem because he felt they would not strengthen faith. "Our faith in him (Christ) was not increased with the visit," he continues. "Before we saw Bethlehem we knew his incarnation; before we saw his tomb we believed in His resurrection from the dead; apart from seeing the Mount of Olives we confessed that his ascension into heaven was real." He also had practical reasons for advising against pilgrimages. Considering the difficulties and discomforts of travel, he was particularly concerned about women pilgrims, who would experience greater hardships "on account of (their) natural weaknesses."

Fortunately Egeria, who arrived in the Holy Land a year after Gregory, did not fear the hardships. She displayed a lively interest, along with determination and stamina, in her efforts to see as much as could be seen, to see "everything." Moreover, she has left us a spirited and stimulating record of her journeys. And now we are all richer because of her efforts, and better informed about church life in the fourth-century east than we ever would have been without her travels.

St Jerome, who settled in Bethlehem five years after Gregory's visit, agreed with the bishop of Nyssa in some of his writings that life in Jerusalem was not always conducive to faith. In Letter 58 to his friend the monk Paulinas, Jerome

Jerusalem: Via Dolorosa, a traditional pilgrimage route for the "Way of the Cross."

says that in Jerusalem "there is no form of uncleanness that they shun away from." Then he assured the monk that nothing was lacking in his faith if he did not undertake a pilgrimage there. "Whether you dwell here or somewhere else you will be judged for your work. . . Forsake cities and their crowds, live on a small patch of ground, seek Christ in solitude." It would be foolish for a monk, according to Jerome, to decide to live among still greater numbers of people than he lived among before in his native country, for "access to the court of heaven is as easy (or difficult) from Britain as it is from Jerusalem," it is the same from the Egyptian as it is from the Judean desert. St Anthony and his monks "have never been in Jerusalem," and yet the door of paradise is opened to them. Only those pilgrims "who bear their several crosses, who day by day rise with Christ and who thus show themselves worthy of the place so holy" will benefit from their pilgrimage.

St Jerome did not believe that the places associated with Christ's life on earth possessed any miraculous or magical powers. They were holy not in themselves, but because of the events that occurred there. He also rejected the supposition that any of these places were "accursed" because of their association with Christ's rejection and crucifixion. In *Letter 46* to Marcella, he called this a "wicked theory," which Christian history, experience and practice refute. He reminded her, as a Roman, that the holy sites in Rome are precisely the places where Peter and Paul shed their blood for Christ. And, he asks, why was Paul is such a hurry to reach Jerusalem (Acts 20:16)? Jerome notes that Christians venerate the tombs of martyrs. "Does the Lord's tomb seem less worthy of veneration?"

Thus, although Jerome recognizes the potential drawbacks of pilgrimages, he also sees many benefits for Marcella were she to decide to join her sisters Paula and Eustochium in Bethlehem: "In our excitement we are already hurrying to meet you . . . We shall together enter the Savior's cave, then shall we touch with our lips the wood of the cross, and rise in prayer and resolve upon the Mount of Olives with the ascending Lord. We shall see Lazarus come forth bound with grave clothes, we shall look upon the waters of Jordan, purified by the Lord's baptism . . . If only you will come, we shall go to see Nazareth . . . We shall make our way to Tabor . . ." Jerome goes on to list Capernaum, the Sea of Galilee, the spot where the five-thousand were filled with five loaves of bread, etc., and all the places which witness to the crucifixion and resurrection of Christ.

Along with many other spiritual seekers over the centuries, St Jerome was enriched by venerating and touching the holy places, for they are sanctified by Christ's presence. The Sea of Galilee was blessed when Jesus traveled across it, the Jordan River was blessed when Jesus was baptized in it. And nearly 1600 years after Jerome, we can attest to the inspiration and excitement found in rediscovering this sacred geography for ourselves.

Some Observations on Modern Israel

As we traveled from site to site, we had opportunities to see the modern country and to talk with its inhabitants, as well as with long-term residents and political observers. Here are some of their comments and our own observations. The traveler brings his own preconceptions and is affected by those he happens to meet. What we say here is tentative and impressionistic; it is offered not as criticism but as a sign of our deep interest in and concern for all those living in modern Israel.

The visitor is struck by the modernity and efficiency of the modern state. Its well-organized airport, the excellent well-marked main roads, the modest but comfortable apartment houses, many with solar heating units on the flat roofs, the sleek air-conditioned bank, the supermarkets and large, attractive tourist restaurants all make the American feel comfortable and at home. The gardens, parks and reforestation projects, and even the public restrooms, well kept under difficult conditions, show care and effective administration. A hundred years ago, under the rule of the Ottoman Turks, much of Palestine was a poverty-stricken desert, and the water of Jerusalem was polluted. During the British Mandate and under the Israelis the situation has been reversed. Sanitation, education and technical progress are at a high level. New projects to irrigate, drain swamps, and harness nature for human betterment are continuing. Looking out from Mount Tabor over the Valley of Esdraelon, you may see the fertile irrigated fields of the kibbutzim, filling the plain of Galilee. The Israelis are also aware of their responsibilities as caretakers of the shrines of many faiths; a substantial amount of their resources goes for archeology, preservation and restoration of monuments.

The traveler notices almost immediately, however, that the Israelis are not the sole claimants to the land they occupy. Guards with long rifles patrol the streets and markets. Military service is universal, and a large proportion of the population is under arms. Some may be friendly and outgoing to tourists, but nevertheless they are protecting what they have gained in war and are pushing to expand their influence over the land. Tanks, army trucks, and airplanes warn of continuous pressure. Once, when we were on the seacoast north of Akko, we saw four jets flying low in close formation right over us toward the north. They were loaded bombers, and soon afterward it was confirmed that they had bombed a Lebanese coastal town.

We never felt ourselves to be in danger, despite the signs of war around us. In part we were affected by the people there, who had lived under the threat of violence for years and had learned to carry on their everyday lives. Danger in this part of the world is a condition of life.

In the occupied zone, in particular, a state of hostility exists between the Israeli occupiers and the Arab inhabitants. In Samaria, for example, Israeli cars are advised to stick to the main highway to avoid being stoned in Arab neighborhoods. Sometimes the Israelis seem to rely overmuch on the armed guards. In Nablus, on the West Bank, we saw a busload of Israeli children with their guards singing patriotic songs on Jerusalem Day, when they were celebrating victory over the Arabs. It seemed unnecessarily provocative to bring children into this completely Arab town on that day.

Israel as a whole is increasingly a segregated society. For example, Jews live only in Upper Nazareth, a new and expanding settlement above the old city which is planned to equal in population lower, Arab Nazareth. Each has its own stores and institutions. Only on the Sabbath, when all stores in Upper Nazareth are closed, the nonreligious Jews come to the shops of lower Nazareth, then withdraw again to their own quarter. When travelers to Israel come under the auspices of one or the other of these peoples, they find it difficult to break through the invisible barriers and establish contact with the other.

Throughout the Occupied Zone in particular, new Jewish settlements were visible on the very tops of hills, surrounded by barbed wire, presumably for the security of the new settlers. The settlements remind the observer of those other fortifiers of strategic hilltops, the Crusaders. We visited Belvoir, an enormous fortress, castle and settlement to the south of Nazareth. This twelfth-century structure incorporated the latest knowledge of military defenses, with outer and inner fortifications and intricate entryways, storage and battle stations, secret stairways, etc. Yet, surrounded by a hostile population and lacking adequate immigration from Europe to support it, the great fortress fell in 1191, only twenty years after it was built, surrendered without a fight.

The Arab population look with hostility up from below at the fortress settlements. At this writing, there are more than seventy such settlements on the West Bank, with a population of twenty thousand. The Israeli policy of coopting new land and establishing more settlements humiliates the Arab farmers who used the land before and fuels continued resentment.

The strain of continued armament and occupation affects the young people in particular. At the Kennedy Memorial Park, on a hill above Jerusalem, we met a high school senior who remarked thoughtfully: "Almost every day military men come to my school and tell us we have the best army and airforce and military equipment. We all like this kind of talk. But when they leave I am not as sure as I would like to be. Outwardly I show confidence in our power, but inwardly I feel fear."

The Jewish population is not as homogeneous as their history might suggest. The role of religion in the Israeli state has been a problem since the beginning, and it seems to be becoming more acute. The Zionists from eastern Europe were secular and socialist in their attitude, and this was the prevailing allegiance in the early years of Israel. The rabbinical parties pressed, with only limited success, for the establishment of a theocratic state, with the installation of rabbinical law as the law of the land. There are signs that the younger generation is becoming more interested in its religious roots.

Sacred Sites

The traditional Jewish sacred site is the Western or Wailing wall, the only part of the retaining wall of Herod's Temple which was not destroyed when the Romans razed it in 70 and 135 A.D. Since the capture of this part of the city in 1967, the Jews are now free to pray here, for the first time since the second century. Celebration here now is a more joyful affair than it was in the recent past. We saw religious Jews praying at the wall. A low opaque screen divides the women's section from the men's. We saw a group of children shouting answers in unison to questions put to them by their religion teacher. Groups of family and friends arrived, presenting boys ready for *bar mitzvah*, which they celebrated with singing and dancing in the great square in front of the wall. The Sabbath service on Friday after sunset attracts tourists and visitors.

The entrance to the Temple Mount itself is above the Western Wall. Religious Jews are forbidden to set foot on the mount, which now contains the sacred sites of Islam. At the gate a sign in Hebrew, English and other languages warns: "Entrance to the area of the Temple Mount is forbidden to everyone by Jewish law, owing to the sacredness of the place," and is signed: "Chief Rabbinate of Israel." In the time of the Temple, only the High Priest entered the Holy of Holies once a year, on the Day of Atonement. As no one is sure where precisely it was located, the whole area is closed to believing Jews.

To pray in one of these sites, which are sacred to several religions, is regarded as a claim to a right. It is particularly sensitive when a representative of the ruling power prays for the first time in a place belonging to another religion, thus asserting a right that had not previously been claimed. In 638, when the Muslim Caliph Omar conquered Jerusalem, the patriarch invited him to pray in the Church of the Resurrection. Omar, however, refused, because he recognized that if he prayed there the ruling Muslims would claim the church for their own. Instead, he ordered prayers just outside the door of Constantine's church, where the Mosque of Omar stands today.

Even now prayer can become an instrument of a political claim. In the autumn of 1981, it was reported that a group of religious Jewish militants attempted to enter the Temple Mount to pray. This move was part of a determined effort to challenge Muslim rights and ownership. The Temple police recognized the act as the basis of a proprietary claim and refused them entrance.

Religious militants also come into conflict with the established practices of the state at archeological sites. Archeologists from Hebrew University who were excavating the City of David, the lower part of Jerusalem, aroused the hostility of religious protesters on the grounds that they were violating the sites of ancient graves. The conflict led to a postponement of the work and attracted worldwide attention. The more fundamentalist and intransigent religious groups have apparently been gaining power in recent years, and as we have already noted, religion plays a more important role for many younger people than it did for the founders of the state.

Jewish Immigration

The immigrants to Israel may be grouped into two major categories: Ashkenazim and Sephardim. The differences between these two groups and their goals is another source of potential strain. The European Jews—the Ashkenazim—who founded the state of Israel, are now confronting Jews from North Africa and Asia—the Sephardim—who come from a different social background. The terms Ashkenazim and Sephardim, which were already known in European experience, evoke different images in modern Israel. In the time of the Moors in Spain the Sephardic Jews there were prosperous and were regarded as more cultivated than Eastern European Jews. But now a reversal has apparently occurred. The East European socialists who built the original kibbutzim and established the ethos and institutions of the modern Israeli state must now come to terms with traders from the Near Eastern marketplace who share few of their values.

The Sephardim resent the all-pervasive interference of the state, which compels them to live in a way that is not congenial for them. They fear that they are being discriminated against because of their lower technical skills and that they will be left behind in the modern industrial state. But an unending stream of newcomers is swelling the ranks of the Sephardim, making the country more and more "Near Eastern." As the *Jerusalem Post* reported while we were there, the Oriental Jews have begun political movements of ethnic protest, trying to get their own candidates elected to the Israeli parliament, the Knesset. The advocates of a unified Israeli state are particularly perturbed by the institutional separatism of these ethnic groups, which fosters resistance to a single legal and moral norm that could be accepted by all Israeli citizens.

Since the capture of Jerusalem in 1967, the Israeli government has been careful to respect the established rights and privileges of foreign religious missions and study centers. Even those wary of them characterize their attitude as "fair." Some uneasiness was expressed about the Israeli practice of requiring that only guides trained in their special schools have the legal right to explain about the holy places to foreign visitors; there was fear that these guides might not respect the religious feelings of pilgrims. All official religions are recognized by the state, and the government even pays teachers of any religion who teach children from families belonging to that faith. The problem here lies in the inadequate preparation of these teachers, who are seldom very effective.

The Israeli government is not much concerned about the attitude of the Christian churches, particularly local Arab Christians, a group of limited influence. Not surprisingly, we heard that they are most concerned about religious organizations which exercise power on the international scene: the Roman Catholic Vatican and the Protestant "moral majority" in the United States.

The Arabs of Palestine

We all have a mental image of what life under military occupation must be like, and we apply these ideas to the conquered Arab population. On closer examination, we find that we must modify our preconceptions and recognize the complexity of the situation.

The Arabs of Palestine are predominantly Muslim, with a large Christian minority. The Christians belong for the most part to the Orthodox Patriarchate of Jerusalem and to the Melchite Patriarchate, which is in union with Rome, as well as to other smaller groups. Within the Muslim majority the Bedouin are separated by their desert origins. There is also a large sect of Druse.

Geography also separates the Arab community. Nazareth and Galilee were an area of Jewish settlement since the early part of the century and became the heartland of the Israeli state. The Arab population there has benefited from the stability and prosperity enjoyed over the last thirty-five years. Solid houses have been constructed in the Arab sections of Nazareth, which is growing rapidly, and business is flourishing. The traffic jams here attest to the general prosperity. In an Arab bank, we saw an elderly man in a fez, who, when he received his bank book back, examined his balance with obvious pleasure. Apparently the visit to the bank was a source of considerable satisfaction to him.

One Christian Arab businessman talked about the idea of a Palestinian homeland, which he advocated. He stressed that he himself would not choose to leave his home in Israeli Galilee and move to such a homeland, however. His concern was for the land which had belonged to Arabs and which the Israelis had confiscated in recent years and were still taking. "We ask for justice to be done," he said, meaning the return of forcibly confiscated land.

The traditional Arab ways of life are being changed not only by Israeli rule but by the modern secular tendencies of urban life that have prevailed world-wide. The importance of consumer goods, x-rated movies in downtown Nazareth, attendance at discos instead of family gatherings or religious services foster the breakup of the traditional social fabric. Institutions such as the family, the church and the mosque are under remorseless attack.

Even religious practices are being modernized. Before dawn the muezzin invites the faithful to prayer, and the visitor cannot miss it. It is carefully recorded, amplified and set to a timer. To some extent one must agree with the remark: "No one is calling and no one is praying."

Many traditional customs are of course maintained by the Arabs, both Muslim and Christian. From our room in Nazareth we heard a long cycle of wedding songs, lasting long into the night. A man's voice, accompanied by the clapping of hands, went on chanting rhythmically for hours, and we would fall asleep only to awake again and hear it still going on. But there was no way for us to tell whether the wedding was Christian or Muslim. For both groups, weddings and funerals are the two rituals that regularly bring large congregations to the church or mosque.

We caught sight of a funeral procession in Nazareth. At least sixty cars in close formation were driving through the narrow streets of the Arab bazaar. A priest was in the first car, and all the others contained only men. We learned that the deceased was an Arab Christian of twenty-three who had been caught under a defective lift in his father's auto repair shop and had been killed.

Whether the deceased is Christian or Muslim, the same mourning period of forty days is observed, during which no member of the family leaves the house. Death is primarily a family matter: church and priest seem to play a subsidiary role in comforting the bereaved.

The Arab woman traditionally marries early and lives a secluded life, spending most of it with other women in the family. Their husbands jealously guard this seclusion, which may reinforce a childlike reaction to the world. A European nun who had worked with some of the young Christian married women in a village near Nazareth said that they were not much interested in Jesus as a historical figure who had lived and worked in their immediate neighborhood, because they thought of him as "God." A more exciting local hero was Elijah, who slew the priests of Baal, and they like the story of St George and the dragon.

We met sophisticated, well-traveled Arab women, as well as attractive and able professional women. Schools and opportunities for girls seem much improved, and many Palestinian Arabs, girls as well as boys, are able and ambitious and make good use of them. It is increasingly difficult for women here to live in isolation, protected from the pressures and opportunities of the modern world.

The prosperity and social change of recent years have also affected the Arabs of the occupied areas. In particular the sharply higher wage scales in Israel have meant well-being for some and social dislocation for others. As Arab tenant farmers are forced off the land, they come to the cities and perform menial work, occupying the role of an underclass in the Israeli state. Many young Arabs, disillusioned with life under occupation and confronting a lack of opportunity, seek to emigrate.

Traditionally the Arabs have had large families, often with two or more wives and many children. "How many children do you have?" I asked an Arab taxi driver. "All together thirteen," was his response. A Muslim in his mid-fifties, he had two wives. "And how many children do you have?" he now asked me. "Two," I said, with the assurance of a man who knows precisely how many he has without numbering them. "Maybe to have two is better," he remarked pensively. "Today everything is very expensive. It is not easy to feed them. And then the wife always asks for something new to put in the kitchen, a new refrigerator or something." In urban life, large families are no longer economically advantageous, but still the high birth rate among them threatens the Jewish majority within the state of Israel. As the Arab population becomes less dependent on agriculture, the traditional family presumably will decrease.

In the city of Jerusalem, the Arab population is steadily diminishing, and the traditional institutions are in decay. Before 1967 the bazaars were reportedly more animated and attractive than we find there today. Still the main thoroughfares of the Arab sections in the Old City, the *souq*, are choked with sellers of rather unimaginative tourist souvenirs, and foreigners are fair game for a hard-sell approach. The negotiations between buyer and seller are carried on by bargaining. The merchant who sets the original price knows that it is not right, considering it only an opening quote from which the bargaining begins. He also knows that you know this, and he expects and respects a good bargainer. If you don't know what you should know and expect, there is no bargaining—only disappointment.

While the bazaar is on the decline, the money changers which Jesus drove from the Temple are still active in Jerusalem. There was a rapid inflation during our visit, and Arab businessmen preferred to be paid in dollars, which could be exchanged as needed outside the Damascus Gate. The rate that the money changers quote is not the same as the official exchange rate, but we were assured that their operations are quite legal.

The exchange rate of the dollar is a matter of vital interest to all who deal with foreigners. On one occasion we were buying some wooden camels from a boy of nine or ten, who was learning English in school. He quoted a price in dollars to us. When we asked what it would cost in shekels, he said: "Then let me see—oh yes, today's exchange is eleven shekels to the dollar." We paid according to that day's exchange rate, as the boy's father proudly watched his son.

Arab Christians are heirs to the Palestinian traditions of continuous Christian worship since the early years of the church. Now their position is becoming precarious. They are reportedly leaving their homeland, especially those living in and around Jerusalem. From the villages of Galilee, where they no longer feel safe, Christians have been moving to the cities because of the rise of Muslim fundamentalism. Visitors and pilgrims from the West, for whatever reasons, ignore these local Christians, whose very survival in the land of Jesus is a miracle in itself.

Orthodox Christians belonging to the Patriarchate of Jerusalem are plagued by a problem of their own. The patriarch and the archbishops who make up the Holy Synod are all Greeks. The faithful, on the other hand, are almost completely Arab. Without an educated clergy and native hierarchs, respected by the Arabs as their own, the Church in this region has little chance of attracting its traditional adherents.

In addition to the tension between Muslim fundamentalists and Christians, there are also conflicts between Muslims and Druse. The visitor to Galilee may have an opportunity to see Druse, for example, who live in about eighteen villages there. There are about 300,000 Druse in the Middle East, most of them living in Lebanon and Syria.

The Druse originated as an Islamic sect in the eleventh century, when some of the followers of the Calif al-Hakim (996-1021) declared him to be an incarnation of the divinity, and taught that in him the One was present. Al-Hakim ruled them as an absolute monarch and was considered to be the infallible Imam. The name of the sect, however, comes from a non-Arab leader of the movement, al-Darazi (d. 1019). They all believe in reincarnation and await the return of al-Hakim.

The Druse have by now become a very closed community, depending exclusively on the loyalty of those born into the sect. No converts are accepted, and no defectors are allowed. The religious teachings are kept secret. Those who are acquainted with the doctrines are known as "the wise," and wear white turbans; all other make up "the ignorant." The initiated participate in Thursday evening services, only in parts of which the "ignorant" are also allowed to worship.

Although the Arab villages on the Golan heights were depopulated following their capture by the Israelis in the 1967 war, the Druse there were allowed to remain. In 1980, the world press reported that the Israeli parliament offered these Druse, numbering over 12,500, Israeli citizenship. This gesture was intended to settle the problem of the occupied territory: the Druse would become citizens, and the land on which they lived would be incorporated into the state of Israel. The Druse, however, were divided by this offer, which brought great tension and split the community. It was not in their interest, some Druse reasoned, to side with Israel on that exposed site. But even those who were convinced that it was better for the area to be under Israel have turned in their identification cards for fear of exclusion from the community. Survival is their primary aim, and throughout the centuries they have survived by solidarity and unity.

The relations between Israeli Jews and Palestinian Arabs shape the experience of life in modern Israel. The thoughtful observer is torn between the arguments of both groups. "If you talk with a Jew," an observer remarked, "he asks you to take his side against the Arabs. If you talk with an Arab he insists you take his side against the Jews. These contacts and conversations are exhausting. But then, in these moments I recall that at the time of Jesus it was not much different. Didn't the Zealots try to bring Jesus many times to their side to support their views and approve their use of force against the Romans? And Jesus resisted these temptations. Instead, he preached the Beatitudes, and emphatically renounced violence."

For Further Reading

Ancient Sources

Cyril of Jerusalem and Nemesius of Emesa. Tr. and ed. W.E. Telfer. Library of Christian Classics, 4. Philadelphia: Westminster Press, 1955.

Egeria's Travels, ed. John Wilkinson. London: SPCK, 1971.

Eusebius. *Life of Constantine the Great.* Nicene and Post-Nicene Fathers, 1.

St Gregory of Nyssa. *On Pilgrimages.* Nicene and Post-Nicene Fathers, 5.

St Jerome. *Selected Works and Letters.* Nicene and Post-Nicene Fathers, 6.

Josephus. *The Jewish Wars.* Tr. G.A. Williamson. New York: Penguin, 1970.

Modern Sources

Aharoni, Yohanan, and Michael Avi-Yonah. *The Macmillan Bible Atlas.* New York: Macmillan, 1968.

Aron, Robert. *The Jewish Jesus.* Maryknoll, N.Y., 1971.

Avi-Yonah, Michael, and Samuel Safrai. "The Temple," *Encyclopaedia Judaica* 15:959-69.

Barrois, Georges A. *Jesus Christ and the Temple.* Crestwood, N.Y.: St Vladimir's Seminary Press, 1980.

Chitty, Derwas J. *The Desert a City: An Introduction to the Study of Egyptian and Palestinian Monasticism under the Christian Empire.* Crestwood, N.Y.: St Vladimir's Seminary Press, 1977.

Cross, F.M., Jr. *The Ancient Library of Qumran.* Grand Rapids, Mich.: Baker Book House, 1980.

Freyne, Séan. *Galilee from Alexander the Great to Hadrian: A Study of Second Temple Judaism.* Notre Dame, Ind.: University Press, 1980.

Hazelton, Lesley. *Where Mountains Roar: A Personal Report from the Sinai and Negev Desert.* New York: Holt, Rinehart & Winston, 1980.

Klinger, Jerzy, "Bethesda and the Universality of the Logos", *St. Vladimir's Theological Quarterly,* Vol 27, No. 3, 1983, pp. 169-185.

Loffreda, Stanislao. *The Sanctuaries of Tabgha.* Jerusalem: Franciscan Press, 1978.

Capharnaum. Jerusalem 1980.

Meyers, Eric M., and James F. Strange. *Archaeology, the Rabbis, and Early Christianity.* Nashville: Abingdon Press, 1981.

Michener, James A. *The Source.* New York: Fawcett Crest, 1965.

Murphy-O'Connor, Jerome. *The Holy Land: An Archaeological Guide from the Earliest Times to 1700.* New York: Oxford, 1980.

North, Robert, and Raymond E. Brown. "Biblical Geography," *Jerome Biblical Commentary* 2:633-52.

Parrinder, Geoffrey. *Jesus in the Qur'an.* New York: Oxford, 1977.

Saunders, Ernest W. "Christian Synagogues and Jewish-Christianity in Galilee," *Explor* 3:1 (1977) 70-7.

Smith, George Adam. *The Historical Geography of the Holy Land.* London: Hodder & Stoughton, 1894.

Valentin, Jacques. *The Monks of Mount Athos.* London: Deutsch, 1960.

Wilkinson, John. *Jerusalem as Jesus Knew It: Archaeology as Evidence.* London: Thames and Hudson, 1978.